The Silk Road: A Very Short Introduction

Very Short Introductions available now:

For more information visit our web site
www.oup.com/vsi/

James A. Millward

THE SILK ROAD

A Very Short Introduction

OXFORD
UNIVERSITY PRESS

OXFORD
UNIVERSITY PRESS

Oxford University Press is a department of the University of Oxford.
It furthers the University's objective of excellence in research,
scholarship, and education by publishing worldwide.

Oxford   New York
Auckland   Cape Town   Dar es Salaam   Hong Kong   Karachi
Kuala Lumpur   Madrid   Melbourne   Mexico City   Nairobi
New Delhi   Shanghai   Taipei   Toronto

With offices in
Argentina   Austria   Brazil   Chile   Czech Republic   France   Greece
Guatemala   Hungary   Italy   Japan   Poland   Portugal   Singapore
South Korea   Switzerland   Thailand   Turkey   Ukraine   Vietnam

Oxford is a registered trademark of Oxford University Press
in the UK and certain other countries.

Published in the United States of America by
Oxford University Press
198 Madison Avenue, New York, NY 10016

Library of Congress Cataloging-in-Publication Data
Millward, James A., 1961-
The Silk Road : a very short introduction / James A. Millward.
p.   cm.
Includes bibliographical references and index.
ISBN 978-0-19-978286-4 (pbk. : alk. paper)
1. Silk Road—History. 2. Silk Road—Civilization.
3. Eurasia—Commerce—History. 4. Trade routes—Eurasia—History.
5. Asia, Central—History. 6. Asia, Central—Civilization. I. Title.
DS33.1.M55   2013
958—dc23   2012036337

7 9 8

Printed in Great Britain
by Ashford Colour Press Ltd., Gosport, Hants.
on acid-free paper

For Herrgottsbescheißerle *and all their cousins*

Contents

List of illustrations

Acknowledgments

My ideas about the silk road in history have developed over years of teaching Central Eurasian history at Georgetown University. First, then, my thanks to students in my classes who, among other things, have gamely attempted to play the *komuz*, drink *kumis*, and even eat *bondegi* in their quest for higher knowledge and better grades. Undergraduates participating in my seminars on the silk road in 2011 and 2012 wrote papers on such topics as lapis, jade, cartography, camels, domes, and dragons. They taught me a good deal. I hope that in time they will learn to love Italo Calvino's *Invisible Cities* as I do.

Many others contributed in diverse ways. Jeffery Popovich and the staff at Lauinger Library provided me with space to work and rapid access to any sources I wanted. Bridget Ansell, a magnificent researcher, found such good material that I often wished this introduction were not so "very short." I'm particularly glad that she reminded me about the three hares. I was privileged to read Valerie Hansen's *The Silk Road: A New History* before publication; her insights, especially on the neglected role of the state in promoting the silk road, have influenced me here. Alison Futrell answered questions on Rome, barbarian queens, and sourcing Latin texts. Christopher Atwood, David Brophy, Al Dien, and Uli Shamiloglu indulged me in a discussion of the words *manti/mantou* in Chinese and various Altaic languages. Michael Green and Sarah Dixon Klump each contributed on the subject of dumplings, and Christine Kim confirmed certain of my observations about Korean picnicking practices. Michelle Wang informed me on art historical questions and anything related to Dunhuang. Javier Puente helped me communicate with the Patrimonio Nacional in Madrid. Katie Knight, general manager of Revolution Cycles in Georgetown, sold me a new tire and provided me with references on ancient Egyptian beer-making. Carol Benedict, Alison Games, David Goldfrank, Sarah Dixon Klump, Jennifer Long, John McNeill, Micah Muscolino, Aviel Roshwald, Song Yi, and Howard Spendelow read all or part of the draft manuscript, and their suggestions have improved the final product. Jeff Wasserstrom introduced me to my editor at Oxford University Press, Nancy Toff, whose uncompromising approach to jargon and verbosity Genghis Khan would have appreciated, as readers no doubt will as well. Mary Sutherland copyedited the manuscript with similar thoroughness, and Joellyn Ausanka shepherded it through production with great efficiency.

I am grateful for financial support from the Center for Eurasian, Russian, and East European Studies at Georgetown that made possible a key trip to Central Asia a decade ago, opening new horizons for me after years of work on the Chinese side of the Pamirs. The nameless Chinese authorities who refused me visas for seven years likewise stimulated my interest in other places, for which I am, in a way, grateful. More recently, the patience of the faculty of Slavic Languages and a summer research fellowship from the Graduate School at Georgetown helped me travel to Moscow and St. Petersburg in 2012, where at the Hermitage and other museums I viewed firsthand many silk road artifacts.

Priya and Maya continue to be diverting—in the best possible way—while Madhulika Sikka remains indispensable to me after more than twenty-five years, and not only because her keen journalist's eye caught an egregious factual error in the first paragraph of my draft.

August 2012
Washington, DC

Chapter 1
Environment and empires

Washington, DC, in June is as hot as many parts of the silk road, though not as dry as the steppes and deserts at the center of the Eurasian continent, from which mountain massifs block moisture from both the Pacific and the Indian Oceans. Its humidity is more like that of India, which the conquerors Alexander and Babur found insufferable, or the lower Yangzi River basin in China, the historical center of silk production. The weather, then, was appropriate enough on the National Mall in June 2002, when the Smithsonian Institution convened a folklife festival dedicated to "The Silk Road."

As the opening ceremonies began in a tent on the long park between the Capitol and the Washington Monument, ventilation fans blew in the scent of dust, hay, and even camels from the transformed Mall. Academics, journalists, embassy representatives, and other special invitees sweated in folding chairs while VIPs perspired on stage: the cellist Yo-Yo Ma, hot but beaming to see the fruition of his project; the Aga Khan, descendant of the prophet Muhammed, Imam of the Shia Ismailis, and festival underwriter, flushed but dignified. Only the featured speaker, the U.S. secretary of state Colin Powell, seemed cool as he stepped smartly to the stage in a crisp shirt and tie. It was less than a year after the 9/11 attacks, U.S. forces were occupying Afghanistan (at the hub of the silk road), and plans for war on Iraq (a major silk-road station) were being hatched only a few blocks away on Pennsylvania Avenue. Aware that at that point Powell remained the only prominent member of the Bush administration counseling against invading Iraq, this particular Washington crowd gave him an enthusiastic ovation. Powell would later change his position, but on that day he spoke convincingly of the Silk Road Festival's keynote themes: "Connecting Cultures, Creating Trust."

The District of Columbia might seem a strange starting point for a silk-road journey. Yet the idea of the silk road—or silk roads—has come to mean many things beyond brocades and caravans, and in its broadest conception, as Yo-Yo Ma and the Smithsonian organizers well knew, it stands for the idea that humanity has thrived most when connected across its far-flung habitats by exchanges of goods, ideas, arts, and people themselves. This understanding of our common world history stresses communication and interactions among peoples rather than differentiation and conflicts between them. Such a viewpoint is certainly ideological, but it is also based on empirical evidence from archaeology and historical texts: from the earliest eras of human habitation in Eurasia, we note signs of migration and trade across the continent; some time after that, we see the synergistic effects of that communication in the mutually reinforcing development of pastoralist and agrarian societies in several regions in Asia, Europe, and Africa north of the Sahara. Agriculture, animal husbandry, metallurgy and other technologies, music, graphic arts, and even religion and political thought—diverse as they are—were not isolated, independent developments of discrete civilizations but different facets of a shared Eurasian project.

Obviously, ancient transcontinental integration does not compare in degree with today's intense global connectivity. But qualitatively speaking, the silk road through history accomplished the same sort of things we attribute to "globalization" today. And our world would be very different without the long-term and ongoing, if not always voluminous or rapid, exchanges that began networking the places we know as Europe, Southwest Asia (the Middle East), Persia, India, China, and Southeast and Central Asia several thousand years ago.

2

Neither silk nor a road

Traditionally, the term "silk road" is used to refer to a road, or roads, between East Asia and the Mediterranean, and spanning the center of the Eurasian continent, a region now known variously as Central Eurasia, Central Asia, Inner Asia, Transoxiana, and sometimes as the 'stans (Afghanistan, Kazakhstan, Uzbekistan, Tajikistan, Kyrgyzstan, and Turkmenistan). We imagine strings of laden camels laboring over that road across grasslands, deserts, and mountain passes, stopping at oasis cities where bazaars overflow with silks and spices. Despite these vivid images, however, it is far from clear exactly what, or where, that "silk road" was.

In November 1997, First Lady Hillary Rodham Clinton visited Kazakhstan, Uzbekistan, and Kyrgyzstan on a goodwill tour. While preparing her remarks for a speech in Kyrgyzstan, one of Clinton's advance people called me at Georgetown University to ask, "Is Bishkek a Silk Road city?" The staffer wanted a simple answer, but the question was not simple. The silk road was not like Route 66—a ribbon of highway spanning a continent. To say what lies or does not lie along it depends on how one approaches silk-road history geographically and chronologically. Bishkek, now capital of Kyrgyzstan, was founded by Russian colonialists in the nineteenth century, renamed Frunze, after a Bolshevik general, in the Soviet era, only to be restored to a version of its earlier name after 1991. It would thus seem too new to be classed as a "silk road" city. Moreover, it lies north of where map makers usually draw their approximations of the silk road; Bishkek is more a steppe and mountain crossroads, whereas such ancient oasis cities as Samarkand or Bukhara are generally considered to epitomize the silk road. Yet to deny silk-road status to Bishkek not only would have robbed Mrs. Clinton's speechwriter of a handy device but would wrongly suggest that neither the steppe routes frequented by nomads nor the modern historical era marked by Russian conquest of Central Asia are part of the silk-road story.

3

1. Eurasia and the silk road

It was a German traveler and geographer, Ferdinand Freiherr von Richthofen (the uncle of Snoopy's nemesis, the "Red Baron" Manfred von Richthofen), who coined the term "silk road." Actually, von Richthofen used the term in both singular (*Seidenstrasse*) and plural (*Seidenstrassen*) in a lecture in 1877 and in his multivolume historical geography, *China* (1877–1912). For him the term referred to routes along which Chinese silk moved from the Han Empire (206 BCE–220 CE) to Central Asia and from which the Han learned

4

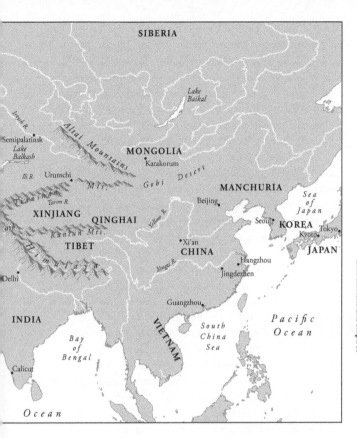

something of western geography. Richthofen did not apply the "silk road" concept to times after the Han period. However, he did discuss at length other routes in later periods and exchanges of goods other than silk; moreover, he argued for the great historical and cultural importance of what he called *Handelsverkehr*, denoting commercial traffic or trade routes. Thus, although in different words, the father of the narrow "silk road" conception was also interested in the general phenomenon of trans-Eurasian exchanges now encompassed by the shorthand we know as the silk road.

The first person to use "silk road" in a title was another German geographer, August Hermann, who published books and atlases relating to the subject in the early 1900s. The title of his 1915 essay, "The Silk Roads from China to the Roman Empire," highlights another common, but misleading, sense attached still today to the silk-road notion: that its importance lay mainly in linking China to the Mediterranean basin, the "east" to the "west." Such a focus on the termini of trans-Eurasian trade is understandable. Our best historical sources from this early period are in fact in Chinese, Greek, and Latin. Moreover, to discover ancient Roman glass in what is now Chinese territory, or to read of Roman ladies sashaying in sheer silks from Serica astounds us, simply because the distances involved are so great. But to focus only on the ends of the silk roads misses the point in several ways.

First of all, the main significance of Eurasian transcontinental exchanges—the phenomenon summed up with the term "silk road"—lies not so much in the trade in silk per se. In fact, there were many things traded and many ideas transmitted across Eurasia, some of which (the domesticated horse, cotton, paper, and gunpowder) had a far greater impact than silk. Moreover, long-distance exchanges continued after they no longer principally involved silk. Conversely, Chinese trade in silk textiles with Central Asian partners closer than the Mediterranean continued unabated into the nineteenth century and remained significant, contributing among other things to the financing of the Manchu Qing Empire's expansion deep into Central Asia, increasing China's territory by a sixth.

Nor should we think the silk road involved only east–west exchanges across the steppe routes at the midpoint of the continent. To do so neglects the region comprising what is now north India and Pakistan, which was not only the transit point for most Han–Rome trade but also contributed such major items as cotton textiles and Buddhism to the Eurasian marketplace of goods and ideas. Likewise, a succession of Persian empires not only facilitated, regulated, and taxed silk-road trade but shaped it through demand for particular goods and cultural contributions flowing east and west. The Persian language, moreover, was for centuries the lingua franca of the silk road.

The narrow conception of the silk road as an east–west route between China and Rome likewise obscures the fact that there was not one "road" but rather a skein of routes linking many entrepôts. Historians think of the silk road more as a network than as a linear route; to map it by simply drawing a couple of horizontal lines across the center of Eurasia and the Indian Ocean, as textbooks tend to do, gives a false impression.

Finally, to focus on contacts between urbanized, agrarian civilizations, while ignoring "the spaces in between"—in British explorer and politician Rory Stewart's phrase—reflects an old bias on the part of farmers and city people across Eurasia with regard to the pastoralist and nomadic inhabitants of Central Eurasia. These people, though often depicted by outsiders as barbarians, were in fact prime historical movers and promoters of silk-road exchanges—"proto-globalizers" as well as conquerors. For example, copper ores exported from the Eurasian steppes in 2100–2000 BCE supplied the Bronze Age metallurgical revolution in Mesopotamia and the Iranian plateau. Chariot warriors, and the technology of the chariot itself, followed the same route. Or, to choose a cultural example, many of the plucked and bowed stringed instruments in European and Asian ensembles today derive from instruments first developed by or with the help of horse-raising peoples of the steppe, and were spread across the continent by Central Eurasian nomads.

Land and man in Central Eurasia

The region known as Central Eurasia is important to us because the silk road spans it, of course, but also because the dynamics of Central Eurasian history, especially the activities

of nomadic herders and their interaction with agrarian states—
the relationship of steppe and sown—shaped trans-Eurasian
exchanges. From prehistoric times, tribally organized speakers
of Iranian, Turkic, Mongolian, and other languages maintained
a pastoralist economy in steppe, desert, and mountain areas
from the Black Sea in the west to Tibet and Mongolia in the east,
bordering on all the Old World's sedentary agrarian civilizations.
The environmental differences between lands inhabited by
farmers and herders was an influential factor in their relationship.

The environment of Central Eurasia can be roughly described as a
series of ecological zones. Northernmost, within the Arctic Circle
in northern Siberia, is the perennially frozen tundra, inhabited
only by the hardiest of reindeer herders and caribou hunters.
South of the tundra is the taiga, a vast band of mainly coniferous
forests circling the globe (oceans excepted) at latitudes that take
in Siberia as well as Manchuria, Canada, and northern New
England, mixing into deciduous forest at its southern edge. Since
this area is poorly suited for agriculture or livestock-raising, the

2. **Central Eurasia**

taiga's main contribution to silk-road history has been fur: minks, ermine, sable, fox, beaver, and other mammals in these northern forests produce dense, rich fur that has long been in demand across Eurasia. Genghis Khan, founder of the Mongol Empire, traded away a wedding present of a sable coat to cement the first major political alliance that propelled him on his road to world conquest. In early modern times, global demand for furs drove Russian trappers eastward across Siberia as far as the Pacific and the frontiers of the Qing Empire, spurring settlement and control of what is now the Russian far east just as French and other European trappers penetrated westward through Canada. Elites in the Qing Empire bought furs from both Siberia and Canada—the "fur road" thus extended to the Americas.

South of the taiga lies the rolling, semi-arid grassland of Eurasia, known by the Russian word "steppe." Near rivers, where irrigation is possible, farming on the steppe could be productive. For the most part, however, humans survived on the grasslands by raising livestock and moving their herds periodically to avoid overgrazing. Because it is mainly dry and flat, crossed by relatively few rivers or major mountain chains, the steppe has also encouraged mobility. Carts can roll on top of it without hardened roads, and horses and other grazing animals move easily over what is to them natural habitat: hard ground covered with their favorite food, like a vast dining table.

South of and interpenetrating the steppe is the belt of Eurasian deserts, starting with the Gobi in southern Mongolia and north China, continuing west through Gansu into Xinjiang's Taklamakan Desert, and the high desert plateau of Tibet to the south. West of the Pamir Mountains, the arid lands pick up again in what is now Uzbekistan and extend south of the Aral and Caspian Seas, along northern Iran and ultimately into the Arabian peninsula and the north African Sahara. Though some of these deserts are composed of shifting sands, others have a hard, pebbly surface. Travel, though requiring a supply of water, could be relatively fast and efficient over such terrain. Polities controlling desert routes often maintained water depots and caravansarays (inns) to help, and profit from, travelers.

Several mountain ranges rise in Central Eurasia, most notably the Kunlun, Tianshan, Karakorum, and Pamir ranges, offshoots of the Himalayan massif that dominates the center of the continent and shapes its climate. Mountains shield Central Eurasia from the Pacific and Indian oceans; and that, combined with high pressure over the highlands, assures that the region gets little rainfall. River systems flowing out of the mountains, including the Amu Darya (Oxus), Syr Darya (Jaxartes), the Tarim, and the Irtysh, were thus the only sources of water for agriculture. The major cities along the central reaches of the silk road lie near these river systems. Though of some use for local transportation, the rivers of Central Eurasia afford no access to the sea. It required a journey across the mountains into north India (today's Pakistan) to bring travelers to the Arabian Ocean, and from there to the Red Sea and Persian Gulf and on to the Mediterranean. This, rather than overland, was the most common channel by which East Asian goods reached Rome and other Mediterranean destinations.

How is this geography related to human society and politics in Central Eurasia and to the economic and other exchanges of the silk road? For centuries, scholars have been intrigued by a historical pattern: at certain points in time, confederations of nomadic tribes came together to raid and extort tribute from or to invade and conquer agrarian lands. At times steppe wars sent great migrations rebounding across the steppe like billiard balls; at other times, the steppe empires extended from one end of the continent to the other. Several explanations have been proposed for these periodic "barbarian eruptions." The earliest theories attribute them to the inherent character of Central Eurasian peoples and the harsh environment they inhabit.

In his *Muqaddimah* (introduction to history), the fourteenth-century Arab scholar Ibn Khaldun argues that not only does environment influence human character but that the motive force and grand cycles of history arise ultimately from where, and how, people live. New tribal confederations, strong of body and infused with "group feeling," come out of the steppes and desert to rule over agrarian lands. These young dynasties, initially strengthened by the abundance and luxury of civilization, eventually grow senile in such soft conditions and are in turn replaced by a new, more vital desert group. Such grand explanatory schemes are today out of fashion. Nevertheless, based as they were on multiple historical cases of just such a revolving door of militaristic tribal regimes in the Islamic world, Ibn Khaldun's observations cannot simply be dismissed.

From a different perspective, the eighteenth-century English historian Edward Gibbon also generalizes about "Scythians and Tartars" (his generic terms for Eurasian nomadic groups). In his *History of the Decline and Fall of the Roman Empire,* he writes:

> The different characters that mark the civilised nations of the globe may be ascribed to the use and the abuse of reason, which so variously shapes and so artificially composes the manners and opinions of an European or a Chinese. But the operation of instinct is more sure and simple than that of reason; it is much easier to ascertain the appetites of a quadruped than the speculations of a philosopher, and the savage tribes of mankind, as they approach nearer to the condition of animals, preserve a stronger resemblance to themselves and to each other. The uniform stability of their manners is the natural consequence of the imperfection of their faculties. Reduced to a similar situation, their wants, their desires, their enjoyments still continue the same; and the influence of food or climate, which, in a more improved state of society, is suspended or subdued by so many moral causes, most powerfully contributes to form and to maintain the national character of barbarians.

Gibbon explains that the military prowess of the Tartars arises from their milk-and-meat diet, their habitation on the steppe, and their practice of the hunt.

Although they use less loaded terms, modern scholars still grant environment a major, if not determining, role in shaping the social, economic, and political dynamics of Central Eurasia. The environment of steppe, desert, and mountain meant that Central Eurasian nomads relied on a herding economy and thus lacked grain, other crops, and many manufactures and luxuries they needed or wanted. They did have horses and equestrian military skills, however, which gave them a military edge over the hot southern agrarian lands where horses could not thrive. This created a dynamic whereby nomad herders interacted with sedentary farmers and city-dwellers by trading or raiding—and often a combination of the two. Due to the danger of overgrazing dry lands, nomads usually lived and herded in small family groups. They maintained ties to larger kin units—the clan and tribe—and myth and historical memory linked them to still larger solidarities, the equivalent of ethnic or national units. At times of crisis or opportunity, nomads could form large, militarily powerful imperial confederations under a ruling elite and common label bearing both ethnic and political meaning, such as Hun, Turk, or Mongol. These confederations could unify vast steppe territories and conquer agrarian states to the south. Gibbon, then, was right that the sociopolitical organization, individual hardiness, easy mobilization for war, and formidable equestrian skills of the nomads were shaped by their environment, though he was of course wrong to consider them unreasoning beings living like quadrupeds in a state of nature. There is an erroneous tendency to view empire-building by rulers from urban-agrarian kingdoms (Alexander, for example) as strategic genius, while treating nomad imperial conquests like natural disasters. It makes more sense to recognize that from the second millennium BCE through the eighteenth century CE, Eurasian nomadic societies and their leaders worked deliberately within both their natural and geopolitical environments to leverage their narrow but potent comparative military advantage over sedentary societies for economic sustenance or gain, and, sometimes, for the purposes of territorial expansion.

Because the nomadic herding way of life was so different from that in cities or in peasant farming villages, it has also been common to draw a stark line between "barbarian" peoples of the steppe and those of "civilized" societies. Gibbon reflects this trend to depict herders as fundamentally unlike agriculturalists, but it is just as prevalent earlier and elsewhere around the Eurasian rim. Consider the description of the Xiongnu (pronounced Hsiung-new, a term related to "Hun") nomads by China's founding historian, Sima Qian (145–86 BCE):

> The little boys start out by learning to ride sheep and shoot birds and rats with a bow and arrow, and when they get a little older they shoot foxes and hares, which are used for food. Thus all the young men are able to use a bow and act as armed cavalry in time of war. It is their custom to herd their flocks in times of peace and make their living by hunting, but in periods of crisis they take up arms and go off on plundering and marauding expeditions. This seems to be their inborn nature. . . . If the battle is going well for them they will advance, but if not, they will retreat, for they do not consider it a disgrace to run away. Their only concern is self-advantage, and they know nothing of propriety or righteousness.

More vociferously racist is the depiction of the Huns by the fourth-century CE Roman historian Ammianus Marcellinus:

> From the moment of birth they make deep gashes in their children's cheeks, so that when in due course hair appears its growth is checked by the wrinkled scars; as they grow older this gives them the unlikely appearance of beardless eunuchs. They have squat bodies, strong limbs, and thick necks, and are so prodigiously ugly and bent that they might be two-legged animals. Their shape, however disagreeable, is human. They have no use for seasoned food, but live on the roots of wild plants and the half-raw flesh of any animal, which they warm a little by placing it between their thighs and the backs of their horses. They have no buildings to shelter them. They wear garments of linen of the skins of field-mice stitched together.

Once they have put their necks into some dingy shirt they never take it off or change it till it rots and falls to pieces. They have round caps of fur on their heads, and protect their hairy legs with goatskins. They are ill-fitted to fight on foot, and remain glued to their horses, hardy but ugly beasts, on which they sometimes sit like women to perform their everyday business and they even bow forward over their beasts' narrow necks to enjoy a deep and dreamy sleep.

But we need not look so far into the past to find negative images of the peoples of Central Eurasia. Think only of the Disney movie *Mulan*, in which the Shan-yu, swarthy and hulking, evil eyes aglow, swarms over the passes with his myrmidon hordes.

Inner Asian empires and the silk road

With such dark shadows cast through the ages to terrorize today's Disney princesses, it is a challenge to rethink the historical role of the peoples and polities of Central Eurasia. But the nomad peoples and polities of Central Eurasia were more than marauding conquerors. Rather, they were essential to trans-Eurasian connectivity in several ways.

First, the line between steppe and sown was not as firmly drawn as Gibbon, Sima Qian, or Ammianus imply, but was in fact politically and culturally fluid. Relations between nomads and the oases cities were often very close, with nomad powers providing protection and facilitating trade for the oases, and of course, exchange of livestock for agricultural products was advantageous to both. Some semi-nomads even farmed a little for part of the year. Herodotus mentions "farming Scythians" near the Black Sea. Even in the far east, where China's Great Wall seems to define an indelible divide between Chinese farmers and northern herders, reading between the lines of Chinese sources of almost any era reveals a more ambiguous distinction on the ground, with ongoing trade, military alliances, intermarriage and all sorts of linguistic and cultural mixing.

Sima Qian tells of a Chinese marquis who allied with the nomadic Rong peoples to attack the king of the Chinese state of Zhou; of a later king of Zhou allied with "barbarians" (in fact, his in-laws) to attack the Chinese state of Zheng; of how the Yiqu tribes built walls to protect themselves from the Chinese state of Qin; and of the Qin queen mother who bore two bastard children following illicit relations with the Yiqu ruler—not an easy thing to do across an existential divide. The most telling example of this early cultural hybridization in what is now north China and Mongolia was an edict by the king of the Chinese state of Zhao that his people should stop wearing robes and switch to trousers, the better to ride and shoot in. Reading Sima Qian's account, one wonders if the distinction between "Chinese" and "barbarian" was made only after the fact, by commentators like Sima Qian himself. And universally across Eurasia the great agricultural kingdoms and empires were controlled for long periods of time by dynasties of northern tribal conquerors, which thus enter the histories of Russia, Anatolia, Mesopotamia, Persia, India, Central Asia, Tibet, China, Korea, and elsewhere. There was no hard boundary between the nomadic herders of Central Eurasia and their agrarian neighbors; Central Eurasians were neither exclusively nomadic nor always pastoralist; and they enjoyed relations of many sorts with urban and farming communities, not all of them violent. They played a prominent role in Eurasian history.

Most important for the silk road, Central Eurasians participated in and influenced transcontinental economic and other exchanges in several ways. Even when not united in a large confederation, common nomads traded at border markets, visited oases to exchange livestock and other pastoral goods in bazaars, and protected—or imposed protection rackets on—merchant caravans. But large nomad empires were especially important for silk-road exchanges. They needed revenue to make up for diverting much of the productive herding population into military duty, to pay for administrative overhead, and so that the ruling khan could distribute largess to clan members and subordinate headmen to maintain their loyalty. Loot obtained from conquest provided some of this revenue, but extracting tributes from conquered peoples and taxing trade were more sustainable in the long run. Not all Central Eurasian states were equally good at making the transition from a revenue stream based on booty to one based on systematic exchange of goods, but many were commercially minded or, if not, retained merchants to work for them. The movements of tribute and trade goods, under control of Central Eurasian empires, drove many silk-road interactions.

When nomad empires maintained relative stability and built communications, this encouraged trade and travel generally: it is no coincidence that the cosmopolitanism of China's Tang dynasty corresponded to an era when Turk influence extended from Mongolia to the frontiers of India and Byzantium, or that the Polos and European missionaries first reached China when Eurasia was under Mongol rule. Nomad states actively partnered with merchant communities, such as the Soghdians, Armenians, Bukharans, or Uyghurs, to deal with sedentary states and provide their regimes with administrative and fiscal expertise. And the consumption choices of nomad elites and commoners shaped what southern states produced and sold. Most spectacularly, the lavish imperial Mongol courts in China, Mongolia, and Persia encouraged the circulation of their favorite trade goods, artworks, and craftsmen from all across Eurasia. Today we may shop in China for silks or knock-off Louis Vuitton. We may not think of the frightening Shan-yu from *Mulan* as doing the same thing, but he and his ilk were key links and even trendsetters in an international commercial chain during the high points of silk-road communication across Eurasia.

Religious realms

Finally, a word about the role religions, monks, and missionaries played on the silk road. Whereas large empires facilitated exchanges along the silk road through political and military consolidation, the spread of religions did the same by creating religious and cultural realms, zones of shared faith and common religious institutions that overlapped and transcended political and even linguistic boundaries. Missionaries often traveled on the same routes or even together with merchants, affording them the promise of divine protection along the way. Monasteries in remote places served as way stations, pilgrimage centers as market towns, and common faith and knowledge of scriptural languages made travel easier for co-religionists far from home. Moreover, many religious personnel were literate and brought texts and high culture with them as they traveled.

Travel and proselytizing by religious figures had several effects. Unlike merchants, who tend to keep commercial intelligence secret, religious specialists wrote about their journeys. Some of our best information on the silk road comes from monks and missionaries. The seventh-century Tang Buddhist monk Xuanzang left a geographical account of the "Western Regions" through which he traveled en route to India; this text formed the core of Chinese geographical knowledge about Central Asia and India for centuries, and later helped the archaeologist Aurel Stein discover ancient cities buried in the Taklamakan Desert. Ibn Battuta traveled in Africa, eastern Europe, the Middle East, South Asia, Central Asia, Southeast Asia, and China in the fourteenth century, encountering Muslim communities everywhere he traveled. His knowledge of Islamic jurisprudence secured him a warm welcome, gifts, work, and even wives almost everywhere he went.

Religions also offered political regimes, especially imperializing nomad states, a cultural package that included a script, bodies of knowledge including scientific and legal expertise, and clerical personnel, in addition to the promise of salvation or enhanced reincarnation. Manichaeism, which arose in the third century CE in Persia, once had adherents from northern China to the Roman Empire (St. Augustine of Hippo flirted with Manichaeism as a youth in the fourth century). Though extinct today, that dualistic

17

religion was adopted by the nomadic Uyghur state in the eighth century, and Manichaean scribes bequeathed to the Uyghurs a version of the Syriac script once used for the Aramaic language. The script was in turn modified to write Mongolian by Uyghur scribes serving the Mongol Empire. The Uyghur-Mongol script was then adapted by the Manchus to fit their own language. These fearsome seventeenth-century conquerors of China wrote in a script descended from that with which the first Christians transcribed the words of Jesus. Ultimately, it was the Manichaean religion that brought the script east.

Finally, much more than religion circulated through religious networks and via the writings of religious figures. The many centuries of early interaction between India and China brought aspects of Indian science, technology, art, and literature to China along with the Buddhist doctrine and iconography. In the Islamic world, even after the caliphs no longer exercised real control over all Islamic lands, the temporal-religious Islamic system and the shared Arabic and Persian languages facilitated the circulation of knowledge over much of Eurasia. In this way, for example, Ibn Sina, working in the Central Asian city of Bukhara, synthesized Hellenic and Islamic medicine into a system later adopted in western Europe. Or, from the sixteenth to the eighteenth centuries, Jesuits brought European astronomy, cartography, mathematics, art, music, and other knowledge to the Chinese court, and transmitted detailed information about China back to a Europe that had hitherto known only the quasi-fabulous tales of Marco Polo. Complementing the unification and infrastructure built by imperial powers, then, religions overlaid a kind of cultural field across large swaths of Eurasia, stimulated communication, and stretched their intellectual connective tissue along the silk roads.

The term "silk road" thus refers to more than just trade in silk between China and Rome over a few centuries. It stands for the exchanges of things and ideas, both intended and accidental, through trade, diplomacy, conquest, migration, and pilgrimage that intensified integration of the Afro-Eurasian continent from the Neolithic through modern times. Warriors, missionaries, nomads, emissaries, and artisans as well as merchants contributed to this ongoing cross-fertilization, which thrived under imperial and religious unifications.

Another major historical cross-fertilization, the Columbian Exchange, occurred when maritime communications were opened between the Old World and the New from the beginning of the sixteenth century. What resulted was an abrupt—in historical terms—and traumatic exchange of germs, plants, animals, and, of course, human populations between Afro-Eurasia and the Americas. That millions of people in the Americas with no prior immunities died from exposure to old-world crowd diseases is just one of the profound effects of the Columbian Exchange.

The silk road had no such clearly identifiable point of departure, and was more in the nature of a growing acquaintanceship than a sudden encounter. But its effects on world history are no less profound for that. By understanding the biological, technological, and cultural commonalities shared across the continent, we see that much of what we consider the intellectual, religious, political, or economic patrimony of "the West" or "the East"—or Christendom or Islam or Europe or Africa or Asia—are actually varied expressions of what was, on a fundamental level, an Afro-Eurasian joint venture.

Chapter 2
Eras of silk road fluorescence

The eras of the most intense silk-road communications were those when not only the sedentary states of the Eurasian rim but also the nomadic confederations on the Eurasian steppe were relatively centralized. Centralized states and confederations promoted trade and diplomacy, and invested in communications and economic infrastructure (secure roads, water depots, inns, reliable coinage, standard weights and measures). They assessed taxes and tributes from travelers and subjects, but it was easier and safer to pay a few larger powers for safe passage than to risk a shakedown or worse from numerous bandit gangs along the way. This chapter introduces the major players of Central Eurasian history who comprise the political context of the silk road.

Early Indo-European nomads (ca. 3000 BCE–300 BCE)

Around six thousand years ago, a community of farmers and herders lived in settlements on the plains north of the Black and Caspian Seas in what is now Ukraine and Russia. The archeological and linguistic evidence indicates that these people spoke Proto-Indo-European (PIE), the ancestor of a large family of languages now spoken in Europe, Iran, and India, including Hittite, Greek, English, and other Germanic languages, Latin and the Romance languages, Russian and other Slavic languages, Farsi, Hindi, Urdu, and many others. Though not the innovators of agriculture and stock-breeding themselves, the first Indo-Europeans were close to the source of these developments in the Fertile Crescent. Moreover, living on the steppe frontier, they had access to horses. After gaining wheel and wagon technology from the Fertile Crescent via the Caucasus, some of these PIE speakers became the first nomadic herdsmen. They moved deeper out onto the steppe, where they encountered non-PIE-speaking horse riders and hunters who adapted the nomadic herding economy from them.

The chronology and mechanism of Indo-European expansion remains controversial, but starting from around the third millennium BCE, various groups of Indo-European speakers began to move south into Anatolia and west to Europe, where daughter languages developed, over time, from PIE. Bronze Age technology, including the chariot, spurred further waves of migration or conquest in the second millennium BCE out of central and northern parts of Eurasia. Indo-European speakers occupied Persia and India. Well into the first millennium CE, Indo-European language branches known as Iranian and Tocharian predominated in Central Asia and even in what is now far western China. Central Asian Persian, known as Tajik, remains a major language in Central Asia today. In fact, thanks to modern European imperialism and the cold-war era influence of the United States and the Soviet Union, an Indo-European language is the primary or secondary official language everywhere in the world except the Middle Eastern Arab lands, China, and some other parts of East Asia.

The first large nomad polity we know of was that of the Indo-European-speaking Scythians (seventh–fourth centuries BCE). They spoke an old Iranian language and were remarkable for presenting a surprisingly unified cultural horizon from the Black Sea to the Altai Mountains in Mongolia. Their tombs, barrow mounds called *kurgans* containing the remains of humans and horses, have preserved ornaments with dynamic portrayals of animals and birds in what is known as the "animal style" of early Eurasian art.

Scythian military skills easily defeated other Iron Age powers. Darius the Great (r. 521–486 BCE), of the Achaemenid dynasty, added both northwestern India and southeastern Europe to his Persian Empire. But Darius nearly foundered when he marched north against the Scythians, despite an army hundreds of thousands strong. To the Persians' surprise, the nomads simply melted away before them. Darius called the Scythian ruler a coward; according to Herodotus his Scythian adversary replied

3. A leather saddle ornament in the shape of a horned tiger from a tomb in Pazyryk in the Altai mountains, sixth century BCE. Artifacts in the vigorous and fantastic "animal style" are found among grave goods from the Scythians and related Iron Age nomad groups all across Central Eurasia. Antlers seem to hold special significance, as horses were buried with masks with antlers attached and common curvilinear decoration seems to derive from antler depictions.

that "in our country there are no towns and no cultivated land, fear of losing which, or seeing it ravaged, might indeed provoke us to hasty battle." His supply lines dangerously overextended, Darius ultimately retreated in ignominy, having fallen for the oldest trick of the Central Asian nomads: the tactical retreat.

The Scythians were more than pastoralists and warriors; they also oversaw the busy trade from the Don and Dnieper basins to the Black Sea, and even supplied grain to the Greeks. Their *kurgans* contain goods from distant parts, evidence of extensive trade relations. The Pazyryk tomb complex in the Altai Mountains held silks, a bronze mirror, and a cup from China as well as a tied carpet probably from Persia or Central Asia. But the Scythian burials are noted mainly for bronze, gold, felt, leather and wood items, and even tattoos in the animal style: predators pouncing on prey, hybrid beasts, and curly decoration reminiscent of elk antlers. The ubiquity of this style speaks to the Scythian cultural reach, from the North Balkans to the frontiers of China.

The classical silk road (third century BCE–third century CE)

The Xiongnu arose somewhat later than the Scythians, in what is modern north China and Mongolia, and conquered territory as far west as modern Uzbekistan. They probably did not speak an Indo-European language but one in the Altaic family from which Turkic and Mongolian tongues would later derive. What we know about the Xiongnu comes mainly from Chinese sources, since the Qin (221–206 BCE) and Han (206 BCE–220 CE) dynasties in China engaged in an off-and-on conflict with the Xiongnu for some 350 years, and events associated with this rivalry helped open the classical eastern silk road. As the Qin consolidated power in what is now north China in the late third century BCE, it drove Xiongnu tribes north and out of their pastures alongside the Yellow River. The Qin walled off the newly conquered territory with "long walls"—the first Great Wall.

A ruthless young prince, Maodun, came to power in the ensuing crisis among the Xiongnu. Using a whistling arrow to indicate his targets, Maodun trained his elite guard to shoot to kill whatever and whomever he commanded. He began by targeting his own favorite horse; when his guard obeyed and shot it, he moved on to his favorite wife, his father's favorite horse, and finally his father himself. As *shanyu*, or ruler, Maodun absorbed or drove off neighboring tribes, attacked the Han to the south, and seized back lands formerly taken by the Qin. Ultimately, the Han emperor was forced to appease the Xiongnu by dispatching Chinese princesses and paying tributes amounting to 200,000 liters of wine, 92,400 meters of silk, and 1,000 ounces of gold annually.

Maodun's successor, Laoshang, smashed the Yuezhi, a powerful nomad confederation in Xinjiang and northwest China. Laoshang fashioned the Yuezhi ruler's skull into a drinking cup, and Yuezhi tribal fragments scattered, some migrating by the mid-second century BCE as far as the northern banks of the Amu Darya in modern Tajikistan and Uzbekistan. Meanwhile, with the Yuezhi gone, the Xiongnu were able to take control over the farming oases in the Tarim Basin (modern Xinjiang), thus securing a source of grain, tribute, and trade revenue.

Despite Han appeasement, the Xiongnu continued their sporadic raids. After nearly sixty years of this, Wu, the new emperor, adopted a more aggressive policy, thus inaugurating more than two centuries of Han struggle with the Xiongnu over the necklace of Tarim Basin oases. Seeking allies and intelligence, in 139 BCE Wu dispatched a minister named Zhang Qian on a mission to Central Asia. The Xiongnu caught him, but after a decade in Xiongnu captivity (where he had children with a Xiongnu wife), Zhang Qian continued west through Central Eurasia to the pastures of the Yuezhi.

Han strategists had hoped the Yuezhi would harbor a grudge against the Xiongnu (who had, after all, turned their king's skull into a drinking cup) and join forces against them. Zhang Qian's diplomacy was to no avail, however, and the Yuezhi stayed put in their new lands. Still, when Zhang Qian eventually made it back to Han territory, he brought intelligence that greatly expanded Chinese geographic, ethnographic, and political knowledge of Central Eurasia, paving the way for later diplomatic and commercial exchanges. For example, his comment that Ferghana (Dayuan) raised "blood-sweating" steeds bred from the so-called horses of heaven stimulated a Chinese demand for these tall and powerful animals. And access to Chinese merchants and goods accompanying subsequent Chinese diplomatic missions to Central Asia launched the centuries-long career of the silk road's most successful merchant guild, the Soghdians. From around Samarkand originally, the Soghdians ultimately worked and lived from the Black Sea to Korea.

The Yuezhi are a prime example of how the silk road mingled nomadic and sedentary peoples and cultures over great distances. Displaced from the Chinese frontier, the Yuezhi and confederated tribes evolved by the first century CE into the Kushan Empire, a state that combined Central Asian nomadic with Persian, Indian, and Hellenic influences, at the hub of the Old World land-and-sea trade routes. In the fourth century BC, Alexander the Great had campaigned into north India and Central Asia. Kushan rule extended over the Hellenized city-states left by Alexander in Bactria (today's northern Afghanistan), as well as the kingdoms of north India, including the vital trade center of Taxila (northwest of Islamabad on the Grand Trunk Road in modern Pakistan) and Mathura farther south. The eastern extent of their influence at times took in Khotan and Loulan in the Tarim Basin, where Kushan documents have been found written in an Indian language called Prakrit. Kushan coins bore Greek or Kharoshthi script along with images of their kings, Greek, Persian, and Hindu gods, and of the Buddha. Reliable coinage helped Kushan broker commercial exchanges between China, India, Persia, and, ultimately, Rome. Kushan became a great patron of Buddhism and promoted the dissemination of the faith through Central Asia, en route to East Asia.

This was the classical era of the silk road, when the Mediterranean basin, Mesopotamia, Persia, Central Asia, and China fell under the centralized control of a handful of empires. Despite the rivalries and wars between the Han and the Xiongnu or between Rome and Parthian Persia—we are told that the Parthian banners at the Battle of Carrhae in 53 BCE were the first silks ever seen by Romans—the development of diplomacy and maintenance of transportation networks stimulated trade, religious dissemination, and a general increase in geographic knowledge across the continent.

A Dark Age? (third–fifth centuries CE)

In the 1930s, the social scientist Frederick Teggart looked at the Eurasian connections between Rome and Han and their shared problem with "barbarians" on the frontiers; he wrote a book attempting to explain what he saw as correlations between Eastern and Western history. Wars in the Roman east and barbarian invasions along the Danube and Rhine were ultimately the result, Teggart argued, of policies of the Han government. How? Through trade and nomadic migrations. Wars in the Tarim Basin disrupted trade that would have passed through Parthia, which in turn made trouble on the eastern Roman frontier in Armenia. Likewise, Han policies to split the Xiongnu set tribes in motion across the steppe to Russia, who in turn drove other "barbarian" tribes before them, right up to the Roman northern frontier in Europe.

Teggart's thesis was a bold attempt at Big History: to get beyond individual nations or even empires and see the global picture. The silk road certainly lends itself to broad-canvas analyses. Moreover, Teggart may have been inspired by the global linkages of World War I and the Great Depression in his own day. Teggart's reach exceeded his grasp: he could not prove that his correlations were not simply coincidences. Nor were the consequences of interrupted luxury trade in the first century really comparable to those of modern trade protectionism, since the economic value of international trade in most old-world economies was miniscule. Still, the parallels across the continent are striking, and the mobility of nomadic tribes was such that major military or political events on one end of the continent could conceivably affect the other.

One intriguing connection concerns the Xiongnu. The words "Xiong" and "Hun" are phonetically related. A Soghdian letter discussing a Xiongnu attack in 316 CE spells the nomads' name as *xwn*—that is, Hun. Were the Xiongnu, then, the ancestors of the Huns who established an empire on the Pontic steppes in the fourth and fifth centuries, invaded northern Europe, and possibly touched off the era of "barbarian" migrations into Europe? There is no evidence of a direct link, but Xiongnu descendents may have made up a ruling elite among the largely Germanic-speaking masses of the Hun confederation. Or the name alone may have been adopted, in much the same way as "Scythian" or "Tartar" became generic terms for Central Eurasian nomadic peoples.

The invasions of Europe by Germanic and other peoples are associated with the long decline and collapse of the western Roman Empire, roughly from the third through mid-fifth centuries. The Han fell in 220 CE, and subsequent politically unstable centuries in north China were a period when "barbarian" peoples entered and built states in the old Han territory. Until recently, it was customary to think of these centuries in China, as in Europe after Rome, as a kind of dark age, but this image is exaggerated. For one thing, powers in Byzantium and Persia remained robust, as were some of the north China states, especially the Tuoba or Northern Wei (386–534), which controlled much of north China for more than a century and maintained close connections with Central Asia even while adopting Chinese institutions and fighting off attacks from other nomads.

Indeed, this period was one of innovation and hybridization, as new conquerors and migrants adopted and adapted the institutions of classical societies. Christianity spread and became institutionalized in Europe and Byzantium; in China, former nomad regimes like the Northern Wei actively promoted Buddhism and other aspects of Indian culture, launching a millennium-long insemination of Indian into Sinic civilization. It was in this period that the cave temples and massive mountainside Buddha carvings in Central Asia and China were constructed or begun: Bamiyan, Kizil, Mogao (Dunhuang), Binglingsi, and Yungang. (Longmen, though stylistically related to these, was carved later, in the seventh and eighth centuries.)

The "decline" and "dark age" paradigms of both European and Chinese history have also led many to assume that the silk road as a whole declined between the third and sixth centuries. But that is true only if we consider contacts between unified Han and the western Roman Empire the only important thing about the silk road. In fact, exchanges on the central reaches of the Eurasian network remained vigorous. In the Tarim basin, largely autonomous oases thrived on agriculture and long-distance trade, much of which was now handled by Soghdian merchants. Indian, Central Asian, and Chinese Buddhist monks translated sutras in monastic centers, including Kucha in the Tarim Basin and Dunhuang on the desert route from China to Central Asia. Kushan kings remained powerful into the mid-third century, after which their place at the Bactrian hub of the silk road was taken by a new tribal confederation, the Hephthalites or White Huns. The Hephthalites contracted Soghdian merchants to bring silk and other luxuries back and forth to Persia, which was now experiencing a golden age under Sasanid rule (224–651). The Sasanids ruled the old Achaemenid and Alexandrian imperial territory in Persia, North India, and north of the Amu Darya (Oxus River) in Transoxiana (Central Asia). Persians thus controlled the nexus of both overland and maritime silk road trade.

Medieval cosmopolitanism (sixth–tenth centuries CE)

By the middle of the first millennium, the most active silk-road integrators were speakers of Iranian languages: merchants under the Sasanids dominated sea trade not only around the Persian Gulf but also in the Arabian Sea, along eastern Africa, coastal India and Sri Lanka, and as far as Malaysia and southern China. Persian merchants inhabited designated neighborhoods in Guangzhou (Canton)—then, as now, an export city. Soghdian merchants fanned out overland to Armenia, throughout Central Asia, across north China, and even as far as Manchuria and Korea. Thanks to the prominence of these groups, Persian would become the lingua franca of silk-road commerce and communication, especially along more southward-lying routes, and would remain so even after the Arab conquests of Persia and Central Asia.

From the mid-sixth century, a new nomadic confederation arose north of China. The Turks were an Altaic-speaking people whose tribal elite took power after rebeling against another nomad state for whom they are said to have worked as blacksmiths. (The spread of the name "Turk" itself is a silk-road phenomenon; the modern nation of Turkey takes its name from the medieval Turks coming out of Mongolia but now has a more diverse population. The first Turks looked rather like Mongolians, Kazakhs, and Kyrgyz do today.) The Turks absorbed neighboring tribes who then took on the political and later ethnic moniker "Turk."

Under its eastern and western khanates, Turk rule extended from Mongolia as far south as Bactria, where it displaced the Hephthalites to control silk bound for Sasanian Persia, and westward beyond the Caspian Sea. Turk power fluctuated over time, confederations fragmented, and the Turk khanates ultimately succumbed to the machinations of the Tang Empire. However, Turkic tribes also influenced the Tang dynasty in China, in particular by manning its armies. Even after the khanates' collapse, the westward migrations of Turkic tribes populated

29

Central Asia with Turkic speakers and led to the formation of several states of great moment to Eurasian history, each of which retained the "Turk" identity and further spread it across Eurasia. These Turk successors included the Uyghur khanate (744–840) in Mongolia and around Turfan, and then a series of powerful regimes providing military muscle and dynastic elites to Persianized Islamic states: the Qarakhanids (999–1211), Ghaznavids (975–1187), Seljuks (1037–1194), Mamluks (1240–1517), Delhi Sultanate (1206–1526), and one could even add the Ottoman (1299–1923), Timurid (1370–c. 1500), and Mughal (1526–1858) dynasties to this broad category of Turko-Irano-Islamic rulers who presided in various territories across the region for nearly a millennium. That so many major states in Central, South, and Southwest Asia shared a common political background and elite culture proved a major factor in silk-road connectivity.

From the seventh to the tenth centuries, another of these Turkic successor states, the Khazar khanate, occupied the North Caucasus and Pontic steppe—a key trade nexus between Black and Caspian Seas, Byzantium, and the Sasanian and later Islamic empires. Furs, honey, and slaves were among the products that came to Byzantium and the Mediterranean from the Volga basin via Khazar territory. The Khazar khans converted to Judaism, possibly influenced by Jewish merchants or exiles fleeing official Zoroastrianism in Persia. The western Turk khanate, too, although its capital was far to the east in the Chu River valley in what is now Kyrgyzstan, enjoyed close diplomatic and commercial relations with the Byzantine court from the mid-sixth century; a Byzantine ambassador to the Turks left a detailed description of the splendor of the western Turk court.

Byzantium engaged with the eastern silk road in order to circumvent Sasanian Persia as a source for silk yarn. Besides working to open direct overland trade with the Turks, Byzantium encouraged Ethiopian merchants to bypass Persia by sea and supply raw silk directly from India. Byzantium developed its own industry for weaving textiles from imported raw silk, and from the mid-sixth century attempted to develop sericulture to supply its own silk thread. Everywhere across the silk road, fine silks took on extra-economic political value, especially as gifts or tributes between monarchs. This was particularly the case in Byzantium, where sumptuary laws blocked silk exports and limited the finest silks to the imperial family and high ecclesiastics. The most restricted fabrics were those dyed the rich purple known as porphyra, with pigment taken from sea snails harvested at the Phoenician port of Tyre.

China was again reunified in this period, first by the Sui (589–618) and then the Tang dynasty (618–906). Tang stands out in Chinese history, not only for its longevity but for the breadth of its territorial expansion. Tang established agricultural colonies in what is now eastern and northern Xinjiang, and temporary military outposts as far as Iran. The dynasty's close if complex relationship to the Turks and its advance into Central Asia contributed to its cosmopolitanism: the Tang capital, Chang'an (modern Xi'an) was home to communities of monks and merchants—Christian, Buddhist, Manichaean, Muslim—from Persia and India as well as Central, Southeast, and Northeast Asia. Chinese taste during the first half of the Tang period embraced objects and culture from the wider world in a manner unprecedented and not to be repeated for several centuries. Tang was also a cultural wellspring for other parts of East Asia, as Han had been before it: aspects of Chinese language, literature, philosophy, music, and political institutions carved a deep imprint on Japan, Korea, and Vietnam. Some of the "Chinese" culture disseminated to East Asia during this period was itself the product of silk-road interactions—the major component is Buddhism, but there are others as well. The tomb of a seventh-century Korean king is designed in the same style as Chinese imperial tombs, with a tumulus mound and approaching "spirit road" flanked by carved stone guards, whose features and dress identify them as Soghdians and Uyghurs. Tang thus conveyed not merely Chinese but also silk-road civilization to other parts of East Asia.

It was also from the seventh century that the Arabs—another nomadic, tribal people—emerged from the desert periphery to conquer much of the Mediterranean and Persian territories of the old Roman and Persian empires. Their expansion was rapid, like Alexander's nine centuries earlier, because they were able to displace an established but crumbling regime: the Sasanians. But the Arabs brought Islam, a potent religious and political ideology, which would have a great impact on the silk road. In particular, after its first dynastic transition, from the Umayyad to the Abbasid Caliphate in 750, Islam extended geographically and ethnically far beyond Arab lands and peoples. The Islamic empire, not surprisingly, absorbed many aspects of Persian political administration and political style, both from Persia and from what Arabs called Mawara'n-nahr, the land beyond the (Amu or Oxus) river, that is, Transoxiana or Soghdia. Despite initial resistance, eastern Persia and Soghdia became integral parts of an ecumenical Islamic world. Indeed, from the ninth to the thirteenth centuries Bukhara was one of Islam's most important artistic and intellectual centers.

In this middle period, then, the Eurasian empires came into direct contact with each other. The Turkic khanate and various Turkic successor states, the Byzantines, and first Sasanian Persians, and then Islamic caliphates shared sometimes violent but commercially active borders and exchanged diplomats and gifts. Tibet, too, became an imperial player, projecting power from its high plateau into the Tarim Basin, Qinghai, western China, and Central Asia, where from the late seventh through the eighth centuries it rivaled the Tang.

This extraordinary constellation of empires brought the Tang, with its mainly Turkic armies, face to face with the Arab, Persian, and Turkic forces of the expanding Islamic empire in Central Asia. The Tang general Ko Sŏnji (a Korean) conquered Tashkent, looted the city, and killed the king; the dead king's son sought aid from the Islamic forces then in Samarkand, and Tang and

Abbasid armies met at the Talas (Taraz) River in 751. Tang lost, although the battle was not of great strategic significance. (The Islamicization of Central Asia and the Tarim Basin was a centuries-long process and was not triggered by this incident. Tang was forced to withdraw its troops from Central Asia not because of Talas but because a rebellion in China in 755 led by An Lushan, a half-Soghdian, half-Turkic general, threatened the capital.) Nevertheless, the Battle of Talas looms large in silk-road history because Chinese captives may have introduced papermaking to Samarkand, whence the technology passed through the Islamic lands and eventually to Europe.

The Mongol world empire (thirteenth–fourteenth centuries)

Genghis Khan (Chinggis Khan, 1162?–1227) has, in the early twenty-first century, been rebranded from bloodthirsty barbarian to something more akin to global visionary. Today's Mongolian nationalists can be forgiven for touting the gathering of the tribes in 1206 that elevated Temujin into the grand khan Genghis as a consultative, democratic forum, nine years earlier than signing of the Magna Carta. But western writers' crediting him with launching the Renaissance or comparing him to Jesus might give some pause.

Why such a radical rehabilitation? A sentence from a student exam essay suggests the reason: "in 1206, Genghis Khan set forth to globalize the known world." The humor of this sentence may have been inadvertent. But were the Mongols, too, engaged in "connecting cultures, creating trust," as the Smithsonian characterized the significance of silk road?

There is a reason for the Mongols' prior reputation. Temujin, a charismatic middle son from the Borjigid clan of the Mongol tribe, became khan only after conquering several other tribes competing for supremacy in Mongolia. After centralizing and reorganizing tribal society, Temujin—now Genghis Khan—embarked on a twenty-year career of conquest in north China and Central Asia. His sons and grandsons eventually expanded the lands under Mongol rule to take in the rest of China, Tibet, Iran, Iraq, and much of Russia, creating a quadrapartite empire consisting of the Yuan in China and Tibet; the Chaghatai khanate in Central Asia; the Il-khanate in Persia and parts of Southwest Asia; and the Golden Horde (Qipchak khanate) on the steppe north of the Black Sea and along the Volga, which exercised overlordship over Kiev and Moscow.

Like other powers before and since, the Mongols used extreme violence for strategic purposes and did not hesitate to raze cities and slaughter populations to set an example for the next city along the way, especially during their early campaigns in Central Asia. Osama bin Laden knew his listeners would get the point when he compared U.S. vice president Dick Cheney to Genghis's grandson Hulegu: the latter is infamous in the Islamic world for executing the caliph, destroying irrigation infrastructure, and sacking Baghdad for seventeen days: the Tigris River first ran black with ink from the city's famed libraries, and then red with blood.

And yet, despite Mongol violence, in a real sense the Mongol Empire unified Eurasia as never before. This unity did not last long. Central Asia was ridden with Mongol internecine strife, and Mongol regimes collapsed in China and Southwest Asia by the mid-fourteenth century; the Golden Horde fragmented early in the fifteenth, with only small successor khantes surviving after 1500. At the empire's height, however, the lands under Mongol rule were linked by familial ties among rulers, a system of mounted communications for official correspondence (the *yam*), shared administrative, legal, taxation, and financial institutions, and a practice of dispatching technocrats and skilled artisans from one part of the realm to the other, especially between the Yuan and Il-khanate, whose relations remained friendly throughout the Mongol period. Relative security made the steppe route from China to the Black Sea ports, and thence to Europe, an economically viable alternative to routes through the Islamic lands: Chinese silk textiles were available in the fairs of Champagne in 1257 for less than the price of silks manufactured in Persia. Just as the Crusades taught northern and western Europe about the Islamic world, the Mongol Empire opened Central Asia and China to European missionaries and merchants. Of the western merchants who during the Mongol period traveled all the way to Cathay, as they called it, the only one who wrote about it was Marco Polo. His geography of Asia, spiced up by the Italian romance-writer to whom he dictated his recollections in a Genoese jail in 1298, proved to be not only a window on the East but also a goad to further exploration: Columbus brought his personally annotated copy of Marco Polo's *Travels* when he sailed for what he thought would be Cathay.

Enclosure of the steppe (sixteenth–nineteenth centuries)

Because the Mongol Empire facilitated Eurasian connections to an unprecedented extent, to some scholars that period marks the beginnings of the modern world. Without going quite so far, it is nonetheless clear that besides intensifying silk road exchanges, the Mongols left a deep impression on the politics and society of Eurasia. Subsequent rulers over steppe and sown were indebted to Mongol tradition militarily, administratively, and in aspects of imperial style. In particular, the Mongols created a hybrid of nomadic and sedentary regimes by going beyond the extractive approach of earlier nomadic empires to rely on systematic taxation rather than only on loot and tribute in agrarian areas. Post-Mongol successor states followed this model.

Royal legitimacy in much of the territories formerly under Mongol rule for centuries afterward hinged on descent from Genghis Khan: only Chinggisids, or descendents of Genghis (Chinggis), could use the title "khan." Timur or Tamerlane (r. 1370–1405), who reconquered much of what had been the western Mongol empire, titled himself *amir* (prince) and "son-in-law," since he himself was not descended from a Chinggisid tribe but simply married a Chinggisid. His own successors left a less martial legacy but one equally reflective of the Mongol foundations. Through the fifteenth century, Timur's heirs presided over a cultural flourishing in Central Asia, Persia, and Afghanistan characterized by a synthesis of Islamic, Persian, and Turkic culture, and marked by high achievement in science (notably astronomy), Turkic and Persian literature, illuminated manuscripts, ceramics, stone carving, and especially architecture: the monumental mosques and madrasas of Samarkand and Herat date from this period. This Timurid renaissance influenced the Tarim Basin oases, Persia, the Ottoman Empire, and India as well.

Babur, the founder of the Mughal dynasty (1526–1757) in India, was a Central Asian of both Timurid and Chinggisid descent, though he primarily valued his Timurid ancestry and even after conquering India still pined for Afghanistan and Transoxiana. The Mughal Empire is a Mongol and Timurid successor state, transplanted to the agrarian rim of Eurasia. But other non-nomadic Eurasian rim states, too, picked up aspects of the Turko-Mongolian tradition. The synthesis of tribal nomadic military power and bureaucratic administration over an agrarian population characterized both the Safavid dynasty (1501–1722) in Iran and the Ottoman Empire (1299–1922). Together with the Mughal Empire, these three states are often called gunpowder empires, attributing their combined military strength and agrarian-based logistical capabilities to the integration of gunpowder weapons into their militaries, with all that entailed with regard to personnel, defensive architecture, and fiscal organization. But besides gunpowder, they were also influenced by Eurasian nomad-type empires. For that matter, a similar argument would include the Ming dynasty in China (1368–1644), which despite its xenophobic reaction to Mongol rule retained aspects of Mongol military organization, was aggressive in its early decades on both steppe and sea, and maintained diplomatic and commercial relations with Central Asia.

Even the tsardom of Moscow (1547–1721) and the Russian Empire (1721–1917) can be characterized as Mongol successors, as can the Qing (Ch'ing) Empire (1636–1911). Both empires ultimately defeated the tribal peoples and khanates of post-Mongol Central Eurasia and absorbed respective parts of the region into their own vast empires; moreover, both combined rule over agrarian and pastoral peoples in Mongol fashion, though they surpassed the Mongols in administrative efficiency, communications reach, and longevity. From one point of view, this amounted to the revenge of the sown over the steppe, a reversal of a balance of power after two millennia. But these early modern empires that enclosed the steppe were also themselves as much heirs to the steppe tradition as they were successors to sedentary empires.

In addition to its debt to Byzantium and Orthodox Christianity, the Russian Empire adopted a number of specific practices and institutions from the Mongols, including certain taxes, military equipment and tactics, and a post-road system based on the Mongol *yam*. Beyond these superficial continuities, one can point to the new development from the mid-fifteenth century of a strong central sovereignty in the person of the grand prince, tsar, or emperor. The ideological roots of tsardom were not directly Central Eurasian: the word "tsar," which the Russians also applied to Mongol khans, derives from "Caesar" and continues the Byzantine tradition of combining supreme secular and church authority in one monarch. Yet the concept of a divinely anointed emperor meshed neatly with Central Eurasian traditions of heavenly khans—as, for that matter, did the Chinese concept of a "Son of Heaven." Russian tsars, moreover, explicitly adopted the model of khanship in their patrimonial relationships with the Kazakhs and other Central Eurasian tribal peoples. To Central Eurasians, the Russian monarch was the "white khaghan" (khan).

The Qing truly was a Mongol successor state, both because its own tribal founders, the Manchus, maintained close relations and intermarried with Mongol tribal aristocracy, and because it consciously manipulated the symbols of Chinggisid legitimacy in its dealings with non-Chinese peoples in Mongolia and Central Asia (where it took over from Mongol rulers). Qing emperors styled themselves "sacred khan" when communicating with Central Eurasians and were great patrons of Tibetan Buddhism as had been the Yuan great khans before them. Besides these ideological techniques, the Qing deployed steppe cavalry financed by China's vast agrarian and commercial tax base to wipe out the Zunghars (another Mongol confederation with imperial ambitions) and add Mongolia, Xinjiang, and Tibet to its holdings in Manchuria and China. Thanks to these conquests, the twentieth-century People's Republic of China is twice the size of sixteenth-century Ming China.

And what of the silk road after the Mongol Empire? It certainly looked different from classical, medieval, or even Mongol eras. After the Qing destroyed the Zunghars, no further steppe-based nomad empires occupied the Central Eurasian "spaces in between." Instead, in the sixteenth and seventeenth centuries Russians advanced across Siberia to the Pacific and to the northern frontiers of Qing, seeking furs for the world market and tea for Russia and Europe. By the seventeenth and eighteenth centuries, Russian demand for cotton textiles and Indian need for horses fueled a sizable trade through Central Asia of which Tashkent and other traditional silk road entrepôts were beneficiaries. The Qing westward expansion into Xinjiang brought Chinese and Central Asian merchants together, and tea, medicinal rhubarb, ceramics, silver, and silks flowed easily across imperial borders. The results of imperial unification in Central Eurasia in the early modern period, then, are like those of earlier silk-road high points: closer connections, expanded mutual knowledge, and increased trade between Russia, India, Persia, Central Asia, and China.

Chapter 3
The biological silk road

Today the main bazaar of Urumchi has been replaced by a shopping center with a Carrefour supermarket and a KFC. But for the statue of a bronze camel in the pedestrian mall outside, it could be anywhere. Until the early twenty-first century, the Erdao Qiao bazaar was a teeming firetrap thronged with shoppers and traders. One section glowed with brilliant textiles, including the Central Asian *etlas* worn by Uyghur and Uzbek women: silks dancing with vertical bands of zigzagging color—or, commonly, polyester versions of the same. And there were strands of fresh-water pearls, stalls of carpets, and trays of bejeweled knives. But this was also a working food market, so local Uyghurs, Han, and Hui (Chinese Muslims) crowded its narrow aisles alongside tourists, ducking under sides of mutton, inhaling the steam from boiling pots of sheep's lung and intestines, and looking over the apricots, almonds, mare's-teat grapes, white raisins, peppers, long beans, tomatoes, green onions, coriander, cumin, chili, and black and green teas.

On my first trip to Erdao Qiao, in 1990, I walked outside the food stalls, across from where Uyghur cooks were grilling mutton kabobs and hooking nan flatbread and mutton-and-onion *samsa* (same word as samosa) out of a clay oven. There, squatting by a wall, were two women instantly identifiable as Kazakhs by their plain-colored headscarves and Turkic features. Between the women, next to a pile of rinds from a melon they'd just consumed, was a grimy ten-liter plastic oil bottle. "Kumis, kumis! Kumis-kumis-kumis!" they shouted. For a few pennies' worth of ragged Chinese banknotes, they unscrewed the lid from the bottle and decanted a frothy off-white liquid into a chipped blue-and-white rice bowl. I sniffed at it with some trepidation. It smelled salty and cheesy; tiny bubbles were rising to the grayish surface. I took a sip, then a mouthful, then drained the bowl.

Kumis—fermented mare's milk—tastes like a savory yogurt drink or a thin, effervescent buttermilk, with a tang of alcohol. I found it intensely refreshing after my push through the stifling bazaar and immediately bought another bowlful.

Historians speak of a "Columbian exchange" of plants and animals that followed the arrival of Europeans in the Americas in the late fifteenth century. Old-world crops, weeds, livestock, and pathogens reworked the landscape and wreaked havoc on American populations in a matter of decades, most dramatically through the epidemics inflicted by old-world germs on native Americans with no prior genetic or acquired tolerances. New-world crops brought to the Old World, among them peppers, tomatoes, potatoes, maize (corn), and tobacco, had effects almost as momentous: China's population and economy doubled in the sixteenth through the eighteenth centuries in part because corn and sweet potatoes from the New World could be grown in marginal land, providing farmers with cheap calories and allowing them to market their rice and other finer grains. Over time the initial European technological advantages diffused to the Americas, and the United States became a relatively early adopter of the package of technological and economic innovations we call the Industrial Revolution.

There was a similar exchange across the silk road, though it was marked not by any sudden contact but by myriad encounters over thousands of years. Although peoples of eastern and western Eurasia were never entirely isolated from each other, nonetheless the long-term trans-Eurasian exchange linked and cross-fertilized what had been distinct Neolithic agrarian systems. Archeologists and historians believe that agriculture developed in China and East Asia independently from the Fertile Crescent, Egypt, and India. Early agriculture in western parts of Eurasia was based initially on wheat and barley cultivation, and that in East Asia on millet and rice. However, since prehistorical times various flora and fauna of use to humans have diffused between these initially distinct poles.

In every corner of the Erdao Qiao bazaar—located at the geographical center of Eurasia—were palpable reminders of trans-Eurasian exchanges both biological and technological. The faces of people milling about, with their Sinic, Turko-Mongolian, and Iranian features, hint at migrations ancient and modern; recent DNA studies corroborate and complicate that story. Many of the vegetables and meats for sale are the product of hybridization of animals and plants from China, India, Persia, and/or Southwest Asia. The cheap blue-and-white ceramic bowl I drank from, though of modern manufacture, reproduces a color and pattern that is Eurasian as much as Chinese, the result of exchanges between the Islamic world, China, and western Europe from the ninth to the nineteenth centuries. And of course the spread of sericulture involved the westward movement of fauna (silkworms) and flora (mulberry leaves) as well as the technology of weaving.

And the horse milk? The domestication of the horse had an impact on human history like that of no other animal, revolutionizing labor, transport, and warfare. This long human/horse partnership began and took its star turn on the Eurasian steppes. The spread of chariot technology across Eurasia is one of the first and best examples of how rapidly, and with what impacts, military technology is diffused.

Even the fact that I was drinking *fermented* milk tells us something: a fascinating story of human natural selection and differing modes of genetic and cultural co-evolution on either end of Eurasia. Lactose-tolerant people have mutations that allow them to keep producing lactase, the enzyme that breaks down the milk sugar lactose, into adulthood. Although these mutations occurred independently in different parts of Afro-Eurasia starting only a few thousand years ago (when humans domesticated cattle), lactase persistence remains most prevalent among populations of northern European ancestry. East Asian populations, on the other hand, have very low rates of lactase persistence, even among nomad herders. But the bacteria that ferment milk break down its lactose into easily digested sugars. Thus fermented milk products (cheese, kumis, sour milk, yogurt, kefir, and so on) feature prominently in the diet of Mongols and Kazakhs. The thirteenth-century European monk-traveler William of Rubruck was struck by the fact that the nomads he encountered drank "sour milk" or *cosmos* (kumis).

Milk alcohol is relatively rare, but most every human culture has developed alcoholic drinks from grains and fruits. Alcoholic beverages in general are an example of convergence: parallel but independent development in different places. But the grapes in the Erdao Qiao bazaar, weighing down arbors in Ferghana or drying into sweet raisins in the hot desert air of Turfan, were imports from the West, and the Eurasian passage of grape wine and its culture from the Mediterranean to ancient and contemporary China is a silk-road story.

Finally, the prepared foods in Erdao Qiao lead us to think about how cuisines have traveled across Eurasia. Noodles and dumplings, found across the continent, may exemplify either diffusion or convergence, but the wheat used to make them was first domesticated in the Fertile Crescent and gradually introduced to north China, where it allowed farmers to grow a third, winter, grain crop. Wheat, not rice or millet, thus became the staple in northern China as in Central Asia. And one particular wheat-based item, the crimped, filled dumpling, may be considered the quintessential silk-road food.

DNA and human migrations

DNA chronology and fossil evidence indicate that anatomically modern humans (*Homo sapiens*) came out of Africa via the Middle East 70,000–130,000 years ago. They followed herds of large mammal prey onto the Eurasian steppes and from there diverged both west and east, supplanting and possibly interbreeding with earlier *Homo erectus* and Neanderthal populations. These travelers were the first silk roadies—and the ancestors of most of us and cousins to modern Africans and more recent migrants from Africa. By 40,000 to 30,000 years ago, humans had migrated to East Asia (new genetic evidence makes it unlikely that East Asians evolved independently in China from a local *Homo erectus* group). Around the time of the last glacial maximum 25,000 years ago, some humans were taking advantage of low sea levels to go to the Americas via northeast Asia and Alaska. Another group had moved earlier, some 40,000 to 60,000 years ago, along the southern tier of Eurasia and via Indonesia to inhabit Australia.

As the last glaciers retreated about 17,000 years ago, the peoples of Eurasia diversified into distinct though not isolated linguistic and cultural communities: the different old-world civilizations. Although the earliest domestications of plants and animals occurred in the Middle East from around 10,000 years ago, different communities across the continent and in the Americas achieved their own independent domestications. Archeological and genetic data show a complex pattern whereby some domestications in Afro-Eurasia (of cattle, for example) took place multiple times independently in different places, whereas other flora and fauna (including the horse) were probably domesticated in one place first, and the domesticated species then diffused through the mechanisms of trans-Eurasian exchange, along with the skills to raise them. This process continued into historical times and still happens today. Xinjiang, of which Urumchi is the capital, became from the 1990s one of the world's largest producers of tomatoes—a new-world crop not known in Eurasia until after 1500 and the Columbian Exchange.

Although still a new field, DNA studies can also inform us, or corroborate what we know from archeological and historical sources about other great migrations across Eurasia including those that shaped the silk road. Scientists studying mitochondrial DNA from human remains found in Kazakhstan have found that samples dating from the seventh century BCE and before contain markers associated with western Eurasian lineages (haplogroups) but none from eastern Eurasia. This tallies with what linguists and archeologists tell us about the westward movements of Proto-Indo-European (PIE) speakers into the deep steppe once they had domesticated horses and adopted wagons. Of course, the Scythians whom Herodotus describes were originally of western Eurasian lineage, as their Iranian language suggests.

The main direction of the first migratory waves during the millennia after the Neolithic Revolution thus seems to have been from west to east. It is no surprise, then, that the well-preserved "mummies" from the Tarim Basin dating from 1800 BCE to 200 CE and now housed in the Museum of the Xinjiang Uygur Autonomous Region look "European" (though neither they nor their ancestors likely came from any farther west than the Black Sea). They share the western Eurasian genetic markers because people from these haplogroups inhabited central Eurasia. Other types of evidence, including names in Greek and Indian sources, and texts dating from centuries later, have led scholars to conclude that at least some of these individuals, when alive, spoke the language Tokharian, an early spinoff from PIE. Tokharian, in turn, can be associated with the Kushan Empire, and possibly with the Yuezhi tribal confederation whom the Xiongnu drove from what is now western China and Xinjiang to Afghanistan and the banks of the Amu Darya.

The analysis of ancient remains in Kazakhstan yielded another discovery as well. Samples from after the seventh century BCE contained an almost half-and-half mix of western and eastern Eurasian haplogroups, along with some Indian-associated haplogroups. Thus the wave that crashed from the west starting around the fourth millennium BCE rolled back again around the middle of the first millennium BCE when peoples of eastern descent expanded westward: Proto-Xiongnu, perhaps, who would be followed by the Turks and the Mongols in the first and second millennia CE. Modern populations of Central Eurasia are highly heterogeneous, with both western and eastern Eurasian markers found in everyone. This is just what we would expect of the peoples of the silk road.

Biological legacies of the Mongols

The Mongol conquest of Eurasia left its own genetic legacy. A unique marker on the Y chromosome in approximately 8 percent of males living in what was once the Mongol Empire, can be traced back to Mongolia between seven hundred and one thousand years ago. The best explanation for this is that one of Genghis's male ancestors from a few generations before him bore a harmless but distinctive mutation on his Y chromosome. Genghis and the dynasties he left after his death carried the same genetic marker, and despite comprising relatively few individuals to begin with, bred so prolifically that they left a vast genetic bootprint across Eurasia. In fact, the Mongol genetic legacy is even larger than this marker on the male line indicates, since we cannot trace Mongol descent through female genetic markers.

Arguably, however, the greatest demographic legacy of the Mongols was not in making people but in eliminating them. This was due not only to their violence and sometime use of massacre as a strategy but to the assistance they lent to *Yersina pestis*: the bacterium that causes plague. Mongols attacking the city of Kaffa in the Crimea in 1346 catapulted corpses of plague victims into the city to speed the siege along. From Kaffa, infected rats, fleas, and people were conveyed by Italian merchants to the

Mediterranean and western Europe. In Europe the Black Death killed one-third of the population; it also wreaked havoc in Iran, Iraq, Syria, Egypt, and North Africa, hitting port and trade cities especially hard.

It was once received wisdom that the Mongols unintentionally brought plague from southwest China to Europe, in the process creating a permanent reservoir for the disease in the snug burrows of marmot and other rodent populations of the central Eurasian steppes, where fleas and plague bacteria could survive cold winters. Plague was in this view a pandemic brought about by the first globalizers. The problem with this theory is that there is no clear evidence that fourteenth-century epidemics in China were plague, or that epidemics of any sort broke out at that time in India or the silk-road cities of Central Asia, through which plague supposedly passed on its way to Europe. Plague is indeed endemic on the steppe, but there is no historical evidence for when it became so—it may well have been there before the Mongol empire.

As with other silk-road stories, genome sequencing provides some new details. The *Y. pestis* samples taken from modern China show the most phylogenetic diversity of samples anywhere—suggesting that China is the site of origin. By some tests, moreover, the oldest strain of the disease is likewise found in China. However, the genome sequencing process identified varieties found in the former Soviet Union as the root of the genetic tree. Thus, though it remains unclear exactly where plague began, we can say that the Mongols unintentionally helped plague get from the Eurasian steppes to northern Europe and the Mediterranean, and possibly from the steppes to north China.

The horse and trans-Eurasian royal culture

In the English-speaking world today, we think of horses with an affection and reverence not unlike that which we afford to dogs. We give horses names; we perceive human attributes in their characters; we design rituals (shows, derbies, fox hunts) around them as markers of elite social class. Horses are not for eating.

Once upon a time in Eurasia, however, our ancestors treated horses as game to be hunted and consumed. Humans must have understood the behavior of horses before we could domesticate them, and this understanding likely arose from the extended contact and observation that comes from hunting a wild herd species. Well after cattle and sheep were domesticated, horses remained wild. In fact, the archeological record does not immediately reveal when horses first were domesticated; while many sites contain equine bones, these might be bones of horses that were either hunted or raised before being eaten.

What perhaps tipped the balance was a climatic change that brought colder winters to Eurasia around the late fifth to early fourth millennium BCE. Horses surpass cattle and sheep at getting food in the winter: they can clear snow off the ground and crack ice covering water sources with their hooves, while other grazers try to use their tender noses. It may have been a need for winter meat under colder conditions that led Eurasians—again, probably on the steppes north of the Black and Caspian Seas—to take mares captive. Sometime after 4800 BCE people successfully bred a stallion with captive mares. The geneticists tell us that all domestic horses in the world today are descendants of that one male. He was probably rather docile, which suited human needs, and given the competition from fierce stallions jealously guarding their harems in the wild, collaborating with humans was perhaps the only way this stallion could get a mate.

The first domestic horses (*Equus ferus caballus*) were kept in herds for meat and possibly milk, and not for transportation. It was once thought that horses were not domesticated until 2500 BCE, and that they were hitched to wagons before being ridden directly. But an ingenious method for measuring tooth wear on pre–Bronze Age horses has shown that horses were being mounted and ridden with non-metallic bits on the Kazakh steppes—probably to hunt other horses—from at least 3700 to 3000 BCE, and possibly earlier than that farther west.

From around 4800 BCE horses appear in symbolic contexts in graves and carvings, first as part of the complex of domesticated animals, but later as representatives of power, virility, or nobility—a role they continue to play. The rise of the chariot cemented their strategic and military importance, although the chariot itself lost its military utility in the first millennium BCE. Horses, with or without chariots, were interred in royal burials: their barrow tombs lie across the Eurasian steppe, in Ukraine, Russia, Kazakhstan, Siberia, and Xinjiang. Herodotus describes a Bronze Age Scythian royal burial with a sacrifice of fifty steeds. Outside Xi'an the tomb of the first Qin emperor is perhaps an amplified echo of the same impulse: besides the thousands of terracotta warriors, his necropolis included terracotta horses and carriages for the emperor himself to ride in the afterworld.

China's relationship with northern steppe peoples and the silk road centered on the horse as much as on silk. Like the Middle East, southern Persia, or India, most of China is poorly suited to raising horses, and stocks needed to be continuously replenished from the Mongolian steppes and Tibetan plateau. These animals were large-headed, shaggy ponies with stiff manes, close to the original wild horse of Asia, *Equus przewalskii* (named for a Russian explorer of Polish ancestry who "discovered" them in the nineteenth century). Przewalski's horse now survives only in zoos and reserves.

In the second century BCE, Zhang Qian reported that Transoxiana "has many fine horses which sweat blood; their forebears were foaled from heavenly horses." This comment inspired a vivid mythology in China about the taller Arab horses, linking them to quasi-fantastical western realms, heaven, and even dragons, from which the best horses were imagined to have been sired. The Chinese poet Li Bai—himself born at a Tang outpost in either

Kazakhstan or Kyrgyzstan—rhapsodized in his "Song of the Heaven Horse (*Tianma ge*)" that "the horses of heaven come out of the caves of the Yuezhi (Kushan), backs tiger-striped, bones like dragon wings." The Han general Li Guangli campaigned as far as Ferghana to bring back a herd of "blood-sweating" horses. Later empires, especially the Tang, received horses from north and west in trade and as diplomatic gifts. After a mid-eighth-century rebellion nearly brought down the dynasty, Tang was forced to purchase horses at an enormous markup from the Uyghur nomads who had come to Tang's aid, paying around forty bolts of silk per head.

Tang needed horses for military reasons, but also because its nomad-tinged aristocracy was strongly invested in what might be called Eurasian royal horse culture, a fascination stoked by exchanges of prize horses with Arab emissaries and reflected in the Tang aristocracy's passion for imperial hunts and polo—even women are depicted in paintings and figurines playing this game. Polo reached China from Persia (where women and kings also played) via the oases of Xinjiang, and from China passed on to Korea and Japan. Meanwhile, Byzantium had likewise learned a version of the game from Iran under the Sasanids, and it remained popular across the Muslim lands after the Islamic expansion. Both Byzantine and Tang palaces had their own polo fields. Like chess, frame-story fables, and the lute, polo is an example of culture emanating from the Persian and Indian center to both European and East Asian silk-road peripheries.

One of the earliest accounts of polo comes from the pre-Islamic Persian national epic, Ferdowsi's *Shahnamah* (Book of Kings). In a highly charged contest between the prince Siyâvosh from Iran (a settled center of civilization), and king Afrâsiyâb from Turan (land of the nomad Turks), historical and civilizational rivals meet on the polo ground:

> Siyâvosh then mounted a fresh horse, threw the ball up out of
> his hand and struck it with the mallet until it appeared to come

49

alongside the moon. You would have said the sky had sucked it up. Afrâsiyâb laughed aloud at the play, and, when the nobles had recovered from their amazement, with one voice they declared that they had never seen so notable a horseman in the saddle. . . . There ensued between the two teams a tussle so fierce that the dust rose up to the sun.

When the British adopted and formalized the "sport of kings" from their Indian dominions in the nineteenth century, therefore, they were drawing from a deep well of Eurasian aristocratic practice. The British royal family still plays the game.

The skills and values of polo are, of course, also those of the hunt and war, especially so when war was prosecuted from horseback. All three activities required equestrian skills, were eagerly practiced by monarchs from one end of Eurasia to the other, and served to mark their elite status. Horses, first herded for meat, became means of transport and made possible the expansion of pastoral nomads out into the deep steppes, where together with camels they enabled the long-distance overland communications of the silk road. Central Eurasian tribal people's comparative advantage in rearing and riding horses ensured their military superiority over settled agrarian societies of the Eurasian rim until as late as the eighteenth century in some places; horses still played a practical martial role through World War I and are still today literally trotted out for state ceremonies because of their associations with warfare, rulership, and power.

The sociologist and economist Joseph A. Schumpeter argued that modern imperialism was driven not by economics, as Marxists believed, but by an objectless desire for conquest on the part of a ruling class socially and ideologically descended from medieval knights. Even in the early twentieth century this aristocracy clung to the psychology and atavistic passions of a bygone time—including horses and the hunt. Arab, Persian, and Mongol horsemen, he wrote, along with feudal European society shared a

similar monarchical identity rooted in war and horsemanship—
that is, "trans-Eurasian royal culture."

Ironically, Schumpeter himself liked to ride, although he was
famously modest about his prowess, at least in the saddle. He
is said to have remarked, "Early in life I had three ambitions. I
wanted to be the greatest economist in the world, the greatest
horseman in Austria, and the best lover in Vienna. Well, I never
became the greatest horseman in Austria."

Grape wine

The silk road gives us many examples of both convergence (similar
phenomena occurring independently in different places) and
diffusion (specific things spreading from one place to another).
Staple grains and cattle were domesticated multiple times in
different places; horse domestication and silk-making technology
developed first in one place but then were eagerly acquired and
diffused elsewhere because they appealed to such universal human
interests as military might, symbolic power, and showy clothing.

The case of alcoholic beverages demonstrates both convergence
and diffusion. All societies that cultivated and stored grain also
discovered how cereals could be fermented in a mash with water,
yeast, and other ingredients to create beers; many places also
fermented fruits into wines. These drinks, in addition to their rich
nutritional content, contained the psychoactive compound ethanol.

Possibly because of our shared physiological reaction to alcohol,
and despite manifold distinct nuances of custom and social
meaning, across Eurasia and the world the consumption of
alcoholic beverages has been associated with some of the same
things. For example, many ancient Egyptian gods and goddesses,
including Osiris and Hathor ("Lady of Drunkenness"), have special
associations with alcohol. Already by the fourth millennium BCE,
ancient Egyptians brewed complex, bready beers and red grape

wine, the former consumed by the masses, the latter mainly by elites. Egyptian tomb and temple paintings frequently depict drinking, and alcoholic beverages featured in funeral rituals. Egyptians may have believed intoxication facilitated communion with the dead and with gods.

Mesopotamians drank beer and wine as well. In the *Tale of Gilgamesh*, an epic tradition for which the earliest known poems date to the beginnings of the second millennium BCE, the harlot Shamhat uses her body and lots of beer to lure the wildman Enkidu out of the wilderness to join humankind. Later, when Gilgamesh seeks a route to the underworld, it is a female tavern-keeper who shows him the way.

In ancient China, too, alcoholic drinks were made from around 4000 BCE, the earliest from grain, and thus a kind of beer (the Chinese word for all alcoholic beverages, *jiu*, is often mistranslated as "wine"). Alcohol was critical in ritual sacrifices to ancestors, and several varieties of early Chinese bronzes were devoted to the heating and serving of these libations for the dead. In China as elsewhere, drink also served to bring the living together. Toward the end of the Shang dynasty (1600–1046 BCE)—perhaps even contributing to its fall—King Zhou held drinking parties where naked men and women splashed after each other in a swimming pool filled with *jiu*. While alcoholic beverages were invented independently in many different places, then it is fair to say they have been commonly associated to one degree or another with conviviality, love, and transcendence.

But grape wine—in particular that made from *Vitis vinifera* subsp. *sylvestris*, the domesticated grape vine—was not universal, at least not at first. Its eventual ubiquity across Eurasia is a product of silk-road diffusion. Just as sericulture started in China and spread west, viniculture began in western Eurasia and moved eastward. Recent DNA research strongly indicates that the grape was first domesticated in the Caucasus during in the Neolithic period (ca. 10,000 BCE). The earliest evidence of domesticated grapes, as opposed to wild grape seeds, has been found in Neolithic sites in what are now Azerbaijan and Dagestan. From there, wine production became fully established by the Bronze Age throughout Mesopotamia and the Mediterranean. Evidence of wine drinking appears in Egyptian tombs from before 3000 BCE and in Greece from 2500 BCE, well before Homer's heroes sailed the wine-dark sea. Viniculture spread to the upland plains of the Karun River and Shiraz highlands in Iran, and wine drinking enlivened Persian culture as well. Herodotus in the fifth century BCE tells us that the Persian elites deliberated over their most important matters while drunk, and would decide the next morning whether to implement their decisions. If they happened to decide on something first while sober, they would reconsider it while drunk. Herodotus likewise mentions that the Scythians drank wine mixed with blood from cups fashioned from the skulls of their enemies (just like the Xiongnu ruler made from his Yuezhi adversary).

North India and Central Asia learned wine culture from Persia and from Alexander's army and camp followers. The Kushan royals in Bactria drank wine from Greco-Roman style *krater* vessels and imported it in amphorae via ports in what is now Pakistan. But Central Asia also produced its own wines. The Roman geographer Strabo writes of Central Asian vintages that could be kept three generations in unresinated casks. Some shrines and monasteries in Bactria have carved scenes and other evidence suggesting that Buddhist monks were making and enjoying wine. In similar fashion, early Christian monasteries in Europe were famous vintners, after the Roman empire spread viniculture throughout their western European territories. When the western Roman Empire fell, the Roman Catholic Church maintained the tradition and technology of wine making through the Middle Ages in order to have wine for the Mass, in which the dark red liquid is understood to transubstantiate into the blood of Christ. The Eastern Orthodox and eastern or "Nestorian" churches (as do those in the Anglican Church) likewise use wine in the Eucharist. The congregation is not meant to become inebriated during such rituals; clearly both western and eastern Christianity, like some early Buddhists and ancient Egyptians,

4. A banquet scene from the first or second century CE, in the Indo-Hellenic style of Gandhara. The woman to the left holds an amphora of grape wine; the man beside her is drinking from a *kylix* wine cup. To the right, musicians entertain on frame-drum and short-necked lute.

recognized this numinous aspect of wine and used it to symbolize and enhance worshipers' connection to God and to each other.

China lay at the eastern end of this chain of transmission. A small Chinese grape may have been fermented in China as early as in the Fertile Crescent and Egypt, but viniculture did not take off in China at that time and grapes remained of minor importance to the Chinese diet. Zhang Qian reported on grapes in Ferghana and brought back grape seeds to plant in the Han capital. But grape wine remained foreign in China, even as it was common in Central Asia. Nonetheless, Chinese liked grape wine when they could get it. In 384 CE Chinese troops under the command of a general named Lü Guang overran Kucha, a cosmopolitan Central Asian oasis and Buddhist center, and "drowned themselves" in its stores of wine. Two and a half centuries later, the Buddhist monk and traveler Xuanzang encountered the fruit of the vine at the camp of the Western Turkic Yabghu, near Issyk Kul (modern Kyrgyzstan). It was a quintessential silk-road tableau: the nomad elites resplendent in embroidered silk brocades, the Yabghu himself in green satin, with a ten-foot silk headband holding back his loose hair. He and his ministers sat on padded mats in a large tent with Xuanzang and a group of envoys from China and Karakhoja (Gaochang, the ruins of which are found today near modern Turfan). The nomads and the envoys listened to a Central Asian band, drank *jiu*, and became increasingly animated, while the abstemious Xuanzang was given sweet grape juice. If the hosts specially furnished the monk with grape juice, it seems likely that what his companions were drinking was grape wine.

A dozen or so years later—in the 640s—viniculture came to China itself. The Yabghu's successor sent a gift of purple "mare's teat" grapes, suitable for making wine, to the Tang court. Yet wine remained exotic, associated with the "west" (Byzantium, Arabia, Persia and Central Asia) even after the Tang conquest of several oases in Xinjiang brought wine-making areas under Chinese control. Karakhoja sent grapes, raisins, and wine to the Tang court as gifts. Cuttings from Karakhoja "mare's-teat" vines were planted in the Tang capital Chang'an (today's Xi'an) and in Gansu in western China. Tang craftsmen decorated bronze mirrors and silk damasks with Hellenistic grape clusters, or made rhyta (Mediterranean-style horn-shaped drinking vessels) or wine jugs in ceramic to resemble Sasanian beaten-silver ewers. One Tang wine vessel depicts a swarthy smiling Soghdian, arms wrapped around a jug as big as he.

The Tang dynasty was also a high point for Chinese poetry, and many verses reference both the silk road and grape wine, which like whirling Soghdians and jangling lutes was closely linked in Chinese eyes with Central Asia. For example, while we might not associate red wine with a drunken soldier, to the eighth-century poet Wang Han, wine set the scene on China's Central Asian frontier:

> Fine grape wine, a jade cup gleaming in the moonlight,
> The pipa urging us from horseback, I drink eagerly.
> Don't laugh if I pass out on this desert battlefield!
> From the march to war, how many have ever returned?

5. This Tang dynasty figurine of a high-nosed foreigner, probably Soghdian, holds a wineskin. Grape wine was associated in China with the "Western Regions"—Central Asia, Persia, and Arabia. Soghdians played an important role in early Tang as traders and intermediaries with nomad groups, from Xinjiang to Manchuria.

That alcohol of any sort instilled a transcendent state of mind is a common theme in Chinese poetry. The same Central Asian Chinese poet Li Bai who wrote about Kushan's heaven horses also loved to drink—16 percent of his poems involve wine. In one well-known verse, he rhapsodizes about drinking alone except for two companions—the moon and his own shadow—from whom drunkenness parts him when he passes out. He concludes the poem by reuniting with them in the Milky Way.

Just as China's relationship with things foreign has at times been ambiguous, the exotic associations of grape wine were not always positive. One nefarious wine drinker was the voluptuous Yang Guifei, consort of the Tang emperor Xuanzong. She is blamed (and was strangled) both for distracting him from affairs of state and for her odd dalliance with An Lushan (Roxshan), the Turkic-Soghdian general. It is very much in keeping with her reputation as femme fatale that she is remembered drinking grape wine from a Roman-style, gem-encrusted glass cup. An Lushan turned on the emperor in 755 and nearly overthrew the Tang. To put down An's rebellion, Tang was forced to withdraw from Central Asia and ultimately took a xenophobic turn, marking the end of a great cosmopolitan epoch in Chinese history.

In the early twenty-first century, as if to make up for centuries of disinterest, grape wine has again become fashionable in China, where it has the advantage of being less intoxicating than rice liquor and thus more convenient for nonstop toasting at banquets. Nor does it hurt that for Chinese, red is an auspicious color. These days Chinese drink around a billion bottles per year, mostly of red wine, and this volume has been growing by 15–20 percent a year for the past decade. China produces hundreds of millions of bottles domestically, with the difference made up largely by imports from France. China buys more Bordeaux than either the United States or Japan.

Just as the Tang was withdrawing from Central Asia, Arab armies and Islam were settling there, having expanded from the Arabian Peninsula through the Middle East, Iberia, Persia, and into Central Asia. Quranic strictures against intoxication are today generally interpreted as banning Muslims from drinking alcohol, and are sometimes treated almost as a central tenet

of the faith or as a primary distinguishing characteristic of
Muslims. These rules, however, have been variously interpreted
in different places at different times. In both Arabic and
Persian literature, the classical poetic genres extolling love and
wine survived after Islamicization, especially in the writings
of mystical Sufis who equated the amorousness and ecstasy
imbued by wine with the longing for union with God and
spiritual transcendence.

Consider the allegorical "Wine-ode" of the thirteenth-century poet
Ibn al-Fārid:

> In memory of the beloved
> we drank a wine;
>   we were drunk with it
> before creation of the vine

> The full moon its glass, the wine
>   a sun circled by a crescent;
>   when it is mixed,
> how many stars appear!

> If not for its bouquet,
>   I would not have found its tavern;
>   If not for its flashing gleam,
> how could imagination picture it?

Wine, here, is a metaphor for religion. Yet for al-Fārid,
connections between love, wine, and faith could be as tangible
as a deep kiss:

> So take it straight,
> though if you must, then mix it,
>   but your turning away
> from the beloved's mouth is wrong.

For the fourteenth-century Persian poet Hafiz (Hāfez), the sensual and spiritual planes intersect still more closely:

> Hair disheveled, face sweating, lips smiling, and drunk;
> garment rent, song-singing, and goblet in hand;
> her eye quarrelsome, lips saying alas,
> last midnight she came to my pillow and sat.
> She brought her head near my ear and in a melodious voice said
> "Are you sleeping, my old lover?"
> A lover who is given such a nocturnal wine
> is a disbeliever in love if he does not become a wine-worshipper.
> Be gone, O ascetic! Find no faults with dreg-drainers.
> For no other gift than this was given to us on the primordial day.
> Whatever He poured into our cup, we drank,
> whether it was the wine of heaven or that of a drunk.
> The laughter of the cup of wine and the curled hair of the beloved—
> O many a repentance like that of Hafiz have they shattered!

Under the Mongols, Islamic and Chinese drinking and religious traditions came face to face, for a short while at least. The Flemish Franciscan monk William of Rubruck traveled overland to the court of the Mongol khan in Karakorum (near modern Ulaan Baator) in the early 1250s. While a guest there, William tried to promote Christianity and had the opportunity to engage in religious debates with Muslims, Buddhists, and Nestorian (eastern) Christians to entertain the khan, the khan's wives, and Mongol courtiers. The courtroom centerpiece, however, was an elaborate bar crafted by a Parisian silversmith in the form of a great silver tree:

> and at its roots are four lions of silver, each with a conduit through it, and all belching forth white milk of mares. And four conduits are led inside the tree to its tops, which are bent downward, and on each of these is also a gilded serpent, whose tail twines round the tree. And from one of these pipes flows [grape] wine, from another *cara cosmos*, or clarified [fermented and distilled] mare's milk, from

another *bal*, a drink made with honey [mead], and from another rice wine, which is called *terracina*; and for each liquor there is a special silver bowl at the foot of the tree to receive it. Between these four conduits in the top, he made an angel holding a trumpet, and underneath the tree he made a vault in which a man can be hid. And pipes go up through the heart of the tree to the angel.

At a blast of the angel's trumpet, concealed servants would pour the various liquors through the appropriate tubes. The Mongols saw no contradiction in sampling the silk road's varieties of drink right along with its flavors of religion. Was the Edenic image of a serpent in a tree of wine the French silversmith's joke?

The full Manti

Besides bacteria, the domesticated horse and wine grapes, thousands of species were exchanged across Eurasia over several millennia. Historical records tell us of some of these transplantations; others we know about because the original species from which domesticates were bred are found wild in only some parts of the continent. These biological exchanges provide a map of sorts to the multidirectional networks that were the silk road. For example, Eastern parts of Asia gave the rest of Eurasia rice, some varieties of millet, buckwheat, sugar cane, soybeans, peaches, almonds, and some citrus fruits. The Mediterranean region and Iran sent back to China other citrus, alfalfa (important for horse-breeding), broad beans (fava beans), peas, turnips, spinach, and the watermelon, which is originally African but known in Chinese as *xigua*, or "western melon," reflecting its arrival via the silk road. The eggplant or aubergine had a particularly peripatetic career, originating small and oval in Southeast or South Asia, moving into south China and India, and from there on to become a staple in Iran and the Islamic world. Later, the larger, elongated purple variety was reintroduced from Iran into China under the Mongols. Many crops were first domesticated in the center of the continent and moved in both directions. These include the Indian domesticates lemons, cotton (which entered China via Central Asia), and sesame. And surprisingly, several common foods, including carrots from the Himalayas and Hindu Kush, apples from the Tianshan, and possibly even onions and garlic, originated in Central Asia.

One of the most important crops is wheat, which along with barley was domesticated in the Fertile Crescent, where its wild ancestor grasses thrived before the Neolithic Revolution. Wheat and barley entered China around 1500 BCE and, when grown in rotation with rice, allowed Chinese farmers to produce two or even three cereal crops a year. This supported a thriving economy and relatively large population. Even though we often think of China as a rice culture, people in north China have traditionally eaten other staple grains, among which the favorite is hard wheat, consumed in breads, noodles, and other forms.

One of those other forms showed up in a tomb in Astana, outside of Turfan, dating from the seventh or eighth century. It is crimped, crescent-shaped, filled with meat and what looks like chives and lay uneaten for 1,200 years in a wooden bowl underground on the eastern edge of the Central Asian desert: a desiccated dumpling.

Of course, many cultures have dumplings of one sort or another, and the ubiquity of the dumpling in general may be a case of convergence. In Japan, rice dumplings called *dango* are considered "better than flowers" (*hana yori dango*)—because they provide practical nourishment, not just something pretty to look at. In Swabia (southern Germany), clever cooks serve meat ravioli during Lent, it is said, on the assumption that God cannot tell what is in the filling inside that dough. Besides their formal name of *Maultaschen*, these dumplings are called *Herrgottsbescheißerle*, "little god-cheaters."

The Turfan museum dumpling is of a special kind, however, that diffused along the silk road. It resembles a triangular Chinese

61

jiaozi, composed of meat filling crimped into a thin round skin of unleavened wheat flour and boiled or steamed, the kind sometimes called in English "Peking ravioli," or, if fried, "pot-stickers." Yet this food is truly transcontinental: dumplings of this type are found in Japan, Korea, Tibet, Nepal, Afghanistan, Kyrgyzstan, Kazakhstan, Uzbekistan, Siberia, Russia, Armenia, Ukraine, Poland, Latvia, and Lithuania, with similar filled and crimped pastas made in Italy and elsewhere in western Europe. They are stuffed with various things (Chinese like pork; Kazakhs like horse; Russians mix pork, beef, and lamb together; Uyghurs and Uzbeks add pumpkin) and can be served with soy sauce, vinegar, sour cream, yogurt, mint, butter, or the broth they are boiled in.

Not only is this type of dumpling found all along the silk road, but it goes by names that are themselves linked: from Northeast Asia through Central Asia and the Caucasus to Turkey, Turkic and other Altaic languages all use some version of the word *manti;* this is likewise the term used in Afghanistan. In Korea they are *mandu*; in Japan such crescent-shaped dumplings are called *gyoza*, like Chinese *jiaozi*, but Japanese applies the related word *manju* to a variety of stuffed bun. And Chinese has *mantou*: today this is a plain steamed bread, but the word once referred to a meat-filled bun or dumpling. In Russian and several other Slavic languages the word is *pelmeni*—a different word but one with origins in the Siberian language of the Komi people from the Urals. The Komi called these dumplings *pel-nan*, or "ear bread" (for their crescent shape) and would bring them frozen on winter hunting trips to boil up for a quick meal. Thus the Russian name for this favorite food is linked to the tribal peoples of Central Eurasia, just as the words *manti/mantou* preserve a link between China and steppe nomads.

Where did this dumpling originate? China? Italy? Central Asia? Ordinarily temperate European and Asian scholars have descended into heated disputes over whether Marco Polo brought pasta from China to Italy or the other way around. Leaving Marco

Polo out of it (the Turfan dumpling predates him by some six hundred years), even if detailed linguistic analysis determined that Turkic *manti* was originally a loan from Chinese *mantou*, this is still unlikely to establish where something as old and common as this dumpling began. What is clear, however, is that the ubiquity of *manti* dumplings arises ultimately from the diffusion of wheat and owes much to the relationships between sedentary and nomadic peoples from Eastern Europe to Northeast Asia, all of whom have contributed their ways of flavoring and eating them. There's a lot of history wrapped in that little package.

Chapter 4
The technological silk road

Koreans are impressive mountain climbers. Even elderly hikers move fast, heedless of steep rocky terrain or enervating humidity, and seldom stop. They are also professionally outfitted, even on a Sunday excursion to Mt. Bukhansan in Seoul: besides ubiquitous sun visors and bandannas imprinted with maps of mountain temple itineraries, many Korean hikers sport Gore-tex® boots, microfiber quick-dry clothing, ultralight backpacks, CamelBak hydration systems, and retractable molybdenum walking sticks. When they do pause, for lunch, they spread out dish after dish of spiced meats, grilled fish, and multiple vegetable kimchis, all washed down with little green bottles of *soju*—a sweet indigenous vodka. While eating, many sit comfortably on compact folding stools: two rectangles of metal tubing bolted together and pivoting in the middle, a fabric seat stretched across one end.

This kind of camp stool—a classic design, reworked by Koreans in aircraft aluminum—probably originated in North Africa and passed through Central Asia, arriving in China around the second century CE, where it was named, significantly, *huchuang*: "barbarian chair." The *huchuang* was known in Asia from the classical era, but it remained a specialty item, since East Asians did not sit on chairs. The ancient Chinese term we translate as "*chair*man" when we speak of *Chairman* Mao—Mao *zhuxi*—literally means "master of the *mat*," since that's what ancient Chinese sat upon in formal settings. All of which shows that even the most quotidian of "technologies" can have a cross-continental history.

Ancient China was of course technologically capable of making chairs, but it was not until the late tenth and early eleventh century that fixed-frame chairs—with hard platform, back, and sides—became common in Chinese interiors. Before that, the earliest references to chairs in China are Buddhist, first in the representation of seated deities (such as at the Longmen, Yungang, and Dunhuang caves), and then in written advice for monks (meditating on chairs kept them safe from snakes and insects). From there, chairs and thrones were taken up in Chinese courts and only later moved down the social ladder to commoner households. It was thus the centuries of communication between India and China, linked to the spread of Buddhism, that brought the chair to China and encouraged its acceptance as a common household item.

There have been several epochs and axes of intensified communication in silk-road history. The connection between India and China, starting in the first century CE and attenuating only from the mid-ninth century, brought not only Buddhism but also many non-religious ideas and items. For example, in addition to the chair, China adopted, from India, by imperial decree, the technique for producing refined sugar from cane. The explosion of Arab armies out of Arabia in the seventh century and creation of an Islamic empire and zone of cultural influence led to similarly intensified contacts and exchange over much of the middle of the continent. Between the eleventh and thirteenth centuries, the Crusades put Western Europe back in touch with the southern Mediterranean and Persia and led to the reintroduction of classical knowledge, enhanced by Islamic learning, to Europe. The Mongol unification of Eurasia from Korea to Hungary spread military technology as well as aspects of mathematics, astronomy, cartography, agronomy, and other arts and technologies in both directions across the continent.

The silk road owes much to such episodes, and despite its prevalent image as a peaceful highway, these intensified communications arose from war and imperial conquest. Even the Sino-Indian connection, though ostensibly in the hands of Buddhist monks, benefited from Chinese military expansion into Central Asia during the Han and Tang dynastic periods as well as imperial sponsorship of envoys and translation projects. This should not surprise us: the most profound technological exchange of modern times, industrialization, was driven not only by individuals or the market but by states with strategic concerns. This remains true for many new technologies today.

Warp and weft of the silk road

Like horses, silkworms have been domesticated for millennia. Like horses, silk is a product closely associated with Eurasian elites. And as a pair, silk and horses made up one of the most common exchanges on the silk road. In early centuries, Chinese silk fabrics were shipped from east to west, but a longer-lived and ultimately more significant exchange was that of silk (and other) textiles south to north between agrarian and pastoral economies. Horses and silk represent the essence of steppe and sown, the former embodying the martial strength of the Central Eurasian nomads, the latter symbolizing the soft, sensual life of the urbanized elites of Eurasian rimlands. The agrarian lands' need for transport and cavalry mounts was complemented by the nomads' demand for textiles, especially fine silks, which could confer legitimacy and status, and help nomad elites secure their followers' support or be resold for a profit. This contrast and complementarity was a key driver of silk-road history.

The human relationship with silk is intimate, domestic, and feminized. Legend attributes the invention of sericulture to Xi Ling, wife of the mythological Chinese progenitor, the Yellow Emperor. (She supposedly lived in the mid-third millennium BCE, though silkworm cocoons have been found dating from 5000 to 4000 BCE). After accidentally dropping a cocoon into a cup of hot tea, Xi Ling realized that she could unwind it into a long continuous strand. In another story, it was a Chinese princess who, in order to assure herself a supply of silk after her marriage to a Central Asian king, smuggled silkworm eggs and mulberry seeds to Khotan in the first century CE by wrapping them in her headdress. A millennium after that, we are told, Italian women were incubating silkworm eggs in bags nestled between their breasts.

Humans have long intervened directly in the reproduction of the silk moth, *Bombyx mori*, which no longer lives in the wild; nor have the fundmentals of silk production changed much since ancient times. After lovingly guarding and hatching the tiny silkworm eggs (35,000 to the ounce), silk-raising families east and west would light braziers or move out to the barn, yielding their warm houses to larvae in wicker trays in order to protect them from the chill of early spring. Today eggs and larvae are still incubated and fed in trays. *Bombyx mori* larvae voraciously consume the leaves of just one species of mulberry; it takes some two hundred pounds of leaves to produce a pound of silk. Careful sericulturalists supply the caterpillars with leaves day and night for around five weeks until they are almost 3 inches (7–8 cm) long. The caterpillars then spin silk through glands on their heads, which combine fibroin, a protein, with sericin, a gum. Gyrating their heads in a figure-eight motion, the caterpillars wrap themselves into a cocoon wound from a single, strong thread up to 4,000 feet (1,200 m) in length. Throughout this entire period, traditional silk-raising families tended their tiny charges like new parents, avoiding loud noises, keeping them well fed, and clearing waste from the trays. Superstitions once attended this delicate stage in the process: in China, for example, menstruating women were not to enter rooms where the worms were feeding.

Once the cocoons are spun, however, the nurturing is over: before they can emerge as moths, the caterpillars are swiftly killed in their

6. Women in Khotan demonstrate the traditional method of spinning silk. Boiling cocoons in water loosens the strands, which are then spun together into a thicker fiber that can be dyed and woven.

cocoons by steaming or, traditionally, by immersion in boiling water. As the heat dissolves its gum, the end of a filament can be located and unwound. Filaments of five to seven cocoons are spun together to make a thread. Textiles woven from such thread are soft, strong, and easily dyed with more brilliant colors than woolen or vegetable fibers can hold. Silk can be woven into sheer gauze, as were the silks first favored by the Romans, or into heavy patterned damasks.

Ancient Greeks and Romans understood silk to come from a land and people called *Seres*—the source of which term, linguists have recently argued, is none other than the Chinese word for silk (today pronounced *si*) as filtered through Central Eurasian languages. But even though they wore and coveted the fabric, the Romans did not understand the technology behind it. Virgil in his *Georgics* (first century BCE) reflected the common belief that silk thread was combed from leaves; around the same time, the Greek geographer Strabo said that silk was the dried bark of certain trees found in India. A century later, Pliny the Elder still described the silk of the Seres as "the wool that is found in their forests." The Seres, or Chinese, soaked it, combed off its down, and "then to the females of our part of the world they give the twofold task of unravelling their textures and of weaving the threads afresh. So manifold is the labour, and so distant are the regions which are thus ransacked to supply a dress through which our ladies may in public display their charms." It seems that Roman women would modify imported silk fabrics, either by loosening the weave or refashioning it into some kind of lace. Thus, regarding Cleopatra, the Roman poet Lucan wrote that "her white breasts are resplendent through the Sidonian fabric, which, wrought in close texture by the sley of the Seres, the needle of the workman of the Nile has separated, and has loosened the warp by stretching out the web."

Pliny railed against both the transparency and the expense of such textiles. In this he was joined by the philosopher Seneca, who is said to have lamented:

> I see, too, silken clothing—if clothing that can be called, which does not protect, nor even conceal the body—appareled in which, a woman cannot very truly swear that she is not naked. Such tissues are brought to us at enormous cost, from nations so remote that not even their names can reach us; and by the help of this vast expense, our matrons are able to exhibit, to their lovers and in their couches, nothing at which the whole public has not equally gazed.

Such a fuss over caterpillar spit! Yet these eructations of conservative commentators tell us something: silk was new to the Roman empire, its use just then passing from the ruling echelon to a somewhat broader, though still elite, stratum of society. Tiny fragments dating from centuries earlier have been found in northern European sites, but it was not until the last century BCE and first century CE that silk was known and increasingly available in Rome—at this point still traveling all the way from China.

It is wrong to say that Zhang Qian inaugurated the silk road—as we have seen, trans-Eurasian exchanges go back millennia before that. But his trip to Central Asia in search of anti-Xiongnu allies (ca. 129 BCE) did result in an accelerated marketing of Chinese silk in Central Asia, whence it was traded on by way of Bactria (Kushan empire), India, and Parthia. Some, ultimately, ended up in Rome. It was not primarily as a consumer product that Chinese silk moved west, however, but rather as an instrument of imperial policy. The Han empire in these centuries was shipping enormous amounts of silk north to appease the Xiongnu and buy their horses. On a later embassy to a nomadic people known as the Wusun in northern Xinjiang, Zhang Qian brought gold and silk goods worth 100 million *cash* (a Chinese currency unit). Subsequent Han embassies to other Central Asian lands, dispatched to secure big western horses, involved hundreds of people, many of whom, Sima Qian sniffs in his *Shiji*, were

> sons of poor families who handled the government gifts and goods that were entrusted to them as though they were private property and looked for opportunities to buy goods at a cheap price in the foreign countries and make a profit on their return to China.

This simply means that besides official exchange of diplomatic gifts, there was trading on the side, to the irritation of Chinese chroniclers. The next Chinese state to operate extensively in Central Asia, the Tang, likewise used its comparative advantage in silk production for strategic purposes. Tang supported its administration in "the Western Regions" (modern Xinjiang) largely with shipments of silk piece goods—up to 900,000 bolts a year, which were used as currency. Over the years, it delivered hundreds of thousands of bolts of silk to Turks and Uyghurs in what is now Mongolia.

China did not retain its monopoly on all aspects of silk textile manufacturing. Inhabitants of the Tarim Basin understood basic sericultural techniques by the first century CE. Some scholars believe that India was manufacturing silk by the third century CE. Byzantium had silkworms (allegedly smuggled from China in a bamboo pole by Nestorian monks) by around 550 and launched its own silk textiles industry under state monopoly during the reign of Emperor Justinian I (r. 527–565), even while continuing to purchase silk from Egypt and Sasanid Persia. Silkworm cultivation spread to Sicily in the twelfth century and onto the Italian peninsula by the thirteenth century.

Even before then, though, the character of the transcontinental silk trade had changed. By the sixth century, it was not piece goods but silk floss (thread) that was being sold on the east–west continental and sea routes via India. It was woven in the Mediterranean world (for example, in Damascus, hence the word "damask") to match local taste; the best pieces were stained purple with a dye produced from the shells of a Mediterranean mollusk in the Phoenician ports of Sidon and Tyre (modern Lebanon).

Although in later centuries the long-distance east–west silk trade involved fewer piece goods, and the technology of sericulture diffused to most southern parts of Eurasia where the climate could support it, the north–south exchange of silk and other textiles for horses long remained a fundamental economic and strategic dynamic between the steppe and settled agrarian lands. In the eighteenth century, for example, the Mughal Empire was importing as many as 50,000 horses annually from the Central Asian steppes and from Iran to support its cavalry. Indian merchants traded dyes and textiles, primarily cottons from the advanced Indian textile industry, for the Central Asian horses. Many of the Indian products were re-traded in Bukhara and other Central Asian cities, winding up in Russian hands as the Russian empire expanded eastward. This Indian–Central Asian–Russian trade of textiles for horses continued until the nineteenth century, when the British undermined India's textile industry.

And in China, too, the textile-for-horse trade continued through Tang, Song, and Ming dynasties, increasingly supplemented by tea sales as this beverage became a necessity for nomad herdsmen and as Russians, too, developed a taste for it. In the late eighteenth and nineteenth centuries, the Qing Empire launched another massive exchange of silks and cottons with the Kazakhs. Qing imperial officials in northern Xinjiang traded silk from southern China for steppe horses and cotton cloth from southern Xinjiang for sheep and cattle. From 1759 to 1853, the Qing shipped nearly 420,000 bolts of imperial silk from south China to Central Asia. The textile-for-horse trade, the warp and weft of the silk road, extended into modern times.

Silk road or paper route?

Today, as newspapers become digital, millions read "the paper" on small electronic devices; these devices also help us communicate, navigate by map and compass, record and display music and images, read literature, predict astronomical events, perform mathematical calculations, learn market prices, or translate foreign languages. Anyone alive in the late twentieth century and early twenty-first century understands the transformative quality of such technology. Likewise, while silk is the most glamorous silk-road product, paper has had the most impact, since it first revolutionized most of the activities we now do with smartphones. And you can wrap fish and chips in it too.

Paper consists of vegetable fibers that have been beaten and suspended in water and dried on a screen into a felted sheet. Like many things, it was first invented in China, where credit is traditionally given to Cai Lun in the second century CE. Examples have been found, however, from as early as the first century BCE. It was probably first used to wrap things, and only later for writing on (it replaced bamboo strips and supplemented silk textiles and carved tablets for this purpose). But this flexible and strong material was also put to other uses, including as clothing, hats, shoes, armor, kites, as well as one nonliterary purpose still familiar today: a sixth-century Chinese scholar admonished his family not to use scraps of paper inscribed with the classics in the toilet—which demonstrates how inexpensive paper was by that time. (The same issue arose in China during the Cultural Revolution of the 1960s and 1970s: the ubiquity of the words of "master of the mat" Mao made it hard to put old newspapers to an accustomed purpose.)

Buddhism and the Chinese civil service examination system (which relies on candidates' knowledge of the Chinese classics) helped spread paper use to neighboring lands. Korea and Vietnam adopted paper in the first centuries CE; a Korean monk is credited with introducing papermaking to Japan in 610. By then, paper was being made in Karakhoja (Gaochang), but archeologists, including Aurel Stein and Sven Hedin, have unearthed paper documents in Xinjiang dating from centuries earlier. Some are official or commercial records. The Soghdian letters were on paper, including the one describing the fourth-century Xiongnu attacks. Many other paper records, including the earliest printed books and other items from the Dunhuang library cave, concern Buddhism. Oddly, though Chinese missionaries brought paper to India, its use did not catch on there until the twelfth century, after Buddhism's decline in India. Perhaps the humid climate and teeming insect life made paper too ephemeral a medium for religious texts, although later Indo-Islamic texts would indeed use paper.

The Battle of Talas, in which Tang met Arab forces in 751, is reported in a later Arabic source to have been the catalyst for the spread of paper to the Islamic world: Tha'alibi's eleventh-century *Book of Curious and Entertaining Information* records that craftsmen among the Chinese taken captive in that battle opened the first paper mills in Samarkand. Although paper was probably known and made in Transoxiana decades before the Battle of Talas, Samarkand was the first place in the new Islamic world to develop papermaking technology and became famous for its paper exports. Thereafter, paper spread remarkably quickly throughout the lands under the command of the Abbasid caliphate. It is said that Caliph Harun al-Rashid established a paper mill in the capital, Baghdad, in 794/95, to supply paper for his growing bureaucracy. Over the next two centuries, papermaking spread to Syria, Egypt, North Africa, and Spain. Europe learned of paper at this time and imported it from Arab lands, but the first manufacture of paper in Europe was not until the twelfth (Spain) and thirteenth centuries (Italy).

This paper-gap between medieval Christendom and the Islamicate reflects and contributed to differentials in learning and scholarship. The burgeoning production and circulation of books and maps of all sorts in the Islamic world corresponds to the new prevalence of paper from the ninth century. Paper thus spurred scholarship based on the Greco-Roman tradition and Islamic science, but it also had a popular dimension: the earliest extant text of *One Thousand and One Nights* was copied on paper in Egypt or Syria in the ninth century—which suggests that this book, in a relatively inexpensive edition, was to some degree available to common folk. By contrast, even centuries later, the greatest libraries of Europe could boast only a few hundred books in their collections, all on very expensive parchment or vellum (both processed animal skin), and many of them, like those in the Sorbonne, chained to desks.

Of course, what truly disseminated the written word—with revolutionary results, especially in the European Renaissance—was a combination of technologies: paper with mechanical printing. Gutenberg's movable type, with which he produced multiple copies of his Vulgate Bible in 1463–1455, is the well-known European milestone. Like paper, printing technology began in East Asia, where both block printing and movable type were known centuries earlier. Developed on many technological precedents (seals, rubbings, printing on textiles), block printing on paper began around 700 CE in China, and both of the earliest extant examples there are Buddhist: a charm scroll from the early eighth century CE, and the earliest book, a block-printed Diamond Sutra scroll from 868 CE, found at Dunhuang and now in the British Library. It may be that the belief that karma could be accrued by repetition of prayers or copying of sutras stimulated the development of mechanical mass-production methods.

Movable type was invented in China in the mid-eleventh century, and the earliest movable metal type developed two centuries later in Korea—still earlier than Gutenberg. The earliest extant book printed with movable type is Korean (the *Jikji*, a Zen Buddhist primer printed in 1377), but movable type remained of secondary importance in China and East Asia generally. Early movable type could be helpful for printing alphabetic or syllabary scripts, where one needs many of a limited number of different letters. Thus movable type was used for the Uyghur language in an old script derived from Soghdian around 1300. However, the Chinese script, used in China, Japan, Korea, and Vietnam, contains tens of thousands of individual characters, some used frequently, others hardly at all—with the frequencies varying greatly depending on the subject matter of the text. A set of movable type would have to be enormous and still would not fit all needs. It was much more efficient to carve a block in negative—which could print two pages—than to cast, set, and reset pages with thousands of different characters of movable type. Woodblocks also had the advantage of simplifying the integration of text and image on a single page.

Is printing an example of diffusion or convergence? It is not clear whether Gutenberg was inspired by Asian examples when he developed his typographical system. There is a story that his wife, from a Venetian family, had seen Chinese woodblocks at home. On the other hand, Gutenberg combined elements of his technique (ink, ink-pad, type, press) in a unique way. What is without doubt is the travel before Gutenberg's day of printing and printed items over the silk roads from China through the Islamic world and into Europe. The Mongols were instrumental in bringing printed things westward. They adopted a Chinese practice by printing paper money in their domains in Persia in the late thirteenth century. Playing cards are another example. Printed to allow production in quantity, playing cards were first used in China in the ninth century and appeared across the Islamic world over subsequent centuries. By the fourteenth century there are references to them in Europe, where they were possibly brought by the Mongols. Printed religious pictures share a similar timeline and entry point (to Spain and Italy from the Islamic world and to Germany, perhaps due to Mongol activity in Eastern Europe.) In general, the long-distance travel that the Mongol empire facilitated let European missionaries and merchants examine and acquire printed items and write about them in their accounts. Whether the momentous development of European printing arose from a heroic invention, or whether there was a "Chinese background for the European invention of typography" depends largely on one's definition of "invention" and, as for pasta, on the nationality printed on one's passport.

Medicine

Many have noted that in China, medicine and food are not considered separate categories but rather lie along a continuum of things one ingests that have effects on the body. This is often treated as evidence that the traditional Chinese approach to health is more "holistic" than that of modern medicine. Likewise, the philosophy behind traditional Indian Ayurvedic medicine stresses nutrition and consumption of certain foodstuffs to restore "balance" and health. In both traditions, certain foods, though not always the same ones, are understood to be "heating" or "cooling," "wet" or "dry," regardless of physical temperature or juiciness. Flavors and types of food eaten together should be calibrated not just to enhance enjoyment but to ensure the healthiness of the meal. In India, for example, a thin-framed, energetic person whose component parts are dominated by *vata*, a "humor" or *dosha* made up of air and ether, might be cautioned that eating dal (beans) will lead to considerable flatulence. In China, if one is feverish, pears (cooling) are advised, while mandarin oranges or ginger (heating) are not; meats and rich stews are good for sickly people or in cold weather, but one should never eat dog meat (highly warming, especially when cooked with garlic and hot chilies) in the summer months.

We often point to such practices, a combination of traditional textual knowledge and evolving folklore, to distinguish "eastern" from "western" medicine. In fact, however, what they really show us are vestiges of an older, pan-Eurasian medical theory current even in the West until the nineteenth century; it was only then that new discoveries and empirical practices really began to create the body of knowledge that we now know and practice globally as modern medicine.

The idea that foods fall into certain categories based on their "humors" and how they affect the body is shared by ancient Greco-Roman, Indian, Chinese, and Islamic medical traditions. Each tradition has unique indigenous features, but they all express one version or another of what is often called the "humoral theory" regarding the composition and proper functioning of the body. The western version of this scheme derives from the work of Hippocrates, later elaborated on by the second-century physician Galen. Here, the four humors are understood to be fluids in the body (black bile, yellow bile, blood, and phlegm), associated with the four "elements" (earth, fire, air, water), seasons (autumn, summer, spring, winter), psychological temperaments (melancholic, choleric, sanguine, phlegmatic), bodily organs (spleen, gall bladder, liver, brain/lungs), and various permutations of the qualities hot, cold, dry, and wet. That there is a relationship between this Galenic and Indian humoral theory seems clear, but the exact mechanism of transmission—and even the direction of transmission—remains controversial. Nevertheless, contacts between the Mediterranean and the Hellenic city-states in Central Asia likely played a role.

As for China, *The Yellow Emperor's Classic of Medicine* from the Han dynasty (206 BCE–220 CE) contains no humoral theory, but by the fifth century CE Chinese medical texts discuss illness as the result of corporal imbalances of heat, coolness, wetness, and dryness, and point out which foods contain these qualities. Buddhism, as so often, seems to have been the medium bringing these ideas from India to China. Chinese Buddhist writings on natural philosophy describe the body as comprised of four elements: earth, water, fire, and air—imbalances of which were understood to cause illness. Demons, too, made people sick, as could bad behavior in previous lifetimes—ideas also imported from India. These concepts coexisted with China's own theories involving not "four elements" but "five phases" (wood, fire, earth, metal, and water), that correspond in turn to five flavors (sour, bitter, sweet, pungent, salty), the five senses, and two sets of organs. In the great eighteenth-century Chinese novel *A Dream of Red Mansions/Story of the Stone*, characters fall ill due to demon possession, bad karma, or obsessive thoughts and are treated according to the humoral system. Popular belief in China had thus absorbed Indian medical ideas and reconciled them to ancient indigenous ones, at least as far as the question of balance of humors is concerned. In China today, the notion of "heating" or "cooling" foods remains current. When someone urges you to eat duck broth or lotus seeds and avoid donkey-meat burgers in the summer, the underlying logic of their suggestion is both thoroughly Chinese and a product of silk-road interactions linked ultimately to ancient Greece.

The humoral theory reached northern and western parts of Europe later than it entered China and, as with many other aspects of the classical Mediterranean tradition, did so only after a silk-road sojourn. The Abbasid caliphate, whose capital, Baghdad, was one of the largest and most cultured cities in the world, actively supported preservation and translation of Greek philosophical and scientific texts, including medical works by Galen. Just as the monk Xuanzang learned Sanskrit and traveled to India to gather Buddhist scripture, the ninth-century Arab scholar Hunayn Ibn Ishaq, a Nestorian Christian, learned Greek and went to Byzantium to collect medical texts, including more than a hundred of Galen's treatises. Hunayn was a master translator, rendering these and other works into Syriac and Arabic (some of Galen's writing survived only in Hunayn's translations), thereby laying the foundations for centuries of medical writing in the Islamic world, including that by the Bukharan scholar Ibn Sina, known as Avicenna in Latin. Ibn Sina's *Canon on Medicine*, a synthesis of Islamic and Greek medical learning, was the backbone of the corpus of translated and new medical works that entered Europe from the mid-eleventh century. They passed first through the Italian city of Salerno; there scholars in touch with Byzantium studied the Galenic tradition along with Aristotle and other classical works via the efforts of another translator, Constantine the African. (How critical to world history has been the work of linguists!) The humoral theory and other medical knowledge thus came from classical Greece and Rome to late medieval Europe via Byzantium, Baghdad, Bukhara, and other silk road information entrepôts.

In a way, humoral theory "works": it sometimes correctly identifies the nutritional value of certain foods and their appropriateness for certain conditions. But there is another truly effective medical technique in which the silk road played a role in both invention and dissemination. Smallpox (variola) is one of the deadliest diseases to have originated on the Eurasian continent, probably from a rodent virus that jumped species. The disease afflicted people in Egypt and India from the second millennium BCE, whence it spread elsewhere on the continent, scarring and blinding those victims it did not kill. As a "crowd disease," it was endemic in many densely populated areas, where its mortality rate was close to 30 percent, striking children particularly hard. Those who survived outbreaks, however, were immune for life. Adults in cities and agricultural areas, therefore, were likely to have been exposed to and survived the disease and to have at least some immunity to it. The same was not true, however, for Central Eurasian nomads, whose sparse population and infrequent contact with settled areas meant that most adults had never encountered the disease. Towns and cities, therefore, could be deadly for even the fiercest nomad conquerors.

Possibly for this reason, the first systematic governmental efforts at inoculation to protect against smallpox (by introducing a form of live virus into healthy people) occurred in states with roots on the Eurasian steppes: the Ottoman and Qing empires. The disease was definitively identified as a distinct condition around 500 CE in China, and by Al-Razi in the Islamic world four centuries later (Galen had not noted it). There are some suggestions of inoculation in India in the first or second millennium BCE, but the first clear use is in tenth-century CE China; thereafter it seems that the Chinese practiced various approaches to inoculation (deliberately introducing live virus to stimulate immunity), until by the sixteenth century it was a well-known, if still rather dangerous technique. Versions of the practice were also found in Central Asia and Africa after this period, due either to transmission from China or independent invention. We know that there was a great interchange of medical personnel and information between China and Persia under the Mongol empire.

For the Manchu rulers of China during the Qing dynasty (1636–1911), smallpox posed a political as well as medical challenge. The Manchu military was comprised of tribal Manchus and Mongol allies; the court promoted close diplomatic relations with Mongol princes and the high lamas of Tibet, who were all hesitant to come to the Qing capital of Beijing, lest they contract smallpox. Indeed, the Third Panchen Lama died of the disease following a state visit in 1780. Most important, the Manchu imperial clan itself suffered from the disease. China's longest-lived ruler, the Manchu Kangxi emperor (r. 1661–1722), was chosen as heir and enthroned at a young age in part because he had survived smallpox—which may have been the cause of his father's death. Kangxi developed an inquisitive, eclectic, and empirical mind, and personally experimented in the 1680s with various techniques to safely inoculate his own children as well as elites among the Mongolian units loyal to the Qing. Although the most common Chinese method employed live virus (from powdered pustule scabs), it used scabs only from inoculated people or from those infected by a milder variant of the disease (*V. minor*) rather than those with full-blown smallpox, and did so only after storing the material in a controlled environment for some time. These tricks attenuated the virus, lowering the risk of infection to acceptable levels.

At the other end of Eurasia, a more direct form of inoculation was commonly practiced in the Ottoman empire. The wife of the British ambassador, Lady Mary Wortley Montagu, learned of the technique in Istanbul in 1716–18, inoculated her own family and vocally advocated use of the method in Britain. In a process reflecting the same empirical habit of mind exhibited by the Kangxi emperor but in a public context characteristic of the European Enlightenment, information about inoculation was then propagated through scientific journals of the Royal Society. Experimentation began in the 1720s on prisoners in Newgate prison and on colonials in Boston, and inoculation eventually gained broad acceptance. In 1796 William Jenner discovered the method of vaccination, using cowpox virus, that afforded humans some immunity with no risk of contracting smallpox.

Following a global campaign to modernize and universalize smallpox immunization, the World Health Organization declared the disease eradicated in 1979. This is one of the foremost success stories of twentieth-century international collaboration in public health. But these global efforts had begun much earlier, albeit in a less coordinated fashion, with the emergence and communication of inoculation methods across Eurasia.

Military technology

One of the last outbreaks of smallpox occurred in the port town of Aralsk, in Kazakhstan in the heart of Central Eurasia. The Soviet Union maintained a secret biological weapons facility on Vozrozhdeniye Island in the Aral Sea, and in 1971 a test of aerosolized smallpox worked a little too well: it blew shoreward and infected ten people, three of whom died, and prompted a massive, if secret, immunization campaign. The accident, when finally revealed in 2002, heightened fears that terrorists in the post-Soviet era would obtain similar weaponized variola or other diseases.

Among the greatest concerns of our time is the spread of biological, chemical, or nuclear weapons to other entities besides those powers that already possess them. But if history is any guide, this is a losing battle: few things have diffused as readily and pervasively as new military technology. The incentives for any power to adopt—and negative incentives against not adopting—effective weapons are simply too great. The most prominent example from our time has been, of course, atomic and thermonuclear weapons, which have spread through a combination of direct diffusion of technology (through espionage and technology transfer) and by "stimulus diffusion"—the independent invention by one group on the basis of a concept observed among another, rather than direct import of the thing itself.

After the United States developed and first used nuclear devices in 1945, the Soviet Union tested a nuclear weapon in 1949 (in Semipalatinsk, in Central Asia); Britain and France followed in subsequent years. In what may be one of the most significant "silk road" transfers ever, from 1950 to 1960—the decade of warm relations between the USSR and China—Soviet advisors provided

Chinese nuclear scientists with atomic research facilities, an experimental reactor, a cyclotron, elements of a gaseous diffusion plant, and other technological and financial assistance. Besides socialist fraternity, one factor motivating this aid was the Soviet shortage of uranium, which China had in abundance in mines in Xinjiang. The USSR had packed up a sample atomic bomb with full documentation in 1957 and was about to ship it to the PRC when relations cooled, and the USSR abrogated the transfer agreement. Nevertheless, Chinese scientists went on to develop and test an atomic bomb by 1964 (again in Central Asia, at the Lop Nor site in Xinjiang: the old silk road has been the preferred testing-ground for horrific modern weapons).

Eurasian transfers of military technology are nothing new. It was the diffusion of the equestrian military complex that shaped the linguistic map of the continent and underpinned the unique, long-running military-political system of the nomad states. This began with the domestication of the horse and its use for riding (4200–4000 BCE), along with wheeled ox- or donkey-carts introduced from Mesopotamia, which made deep-steppe nomadism possible (3300 BCE). The next critical technology was the war chariot, developed not in the Near East as was once thought but in Central Eurasia. The earliest chariot burials date from 2100 BCE in the Sintashta and Petrovka sites on the steppes east of the southern Urals, where they are associated with intensive bronze metallurgy.

The chariot is not a cart, as it has only two light, spoked wheels on a single axle, and a cab designed to carry only one or at most three standing riders. It took great skill and much practice to drive two or four horses at speed in such a light vehicle, while firing arrows or hurling javelins at an opponent at the same time. It required heavy investments in metals (bronze) and other hardware to equip an army with chariots. These inputs of time and wealth, as well as the weapons and fine grave goods accompanying chariot burials, show that the steppe societies producing and deploying chariots were stratified, with power centralized in elite hands.

The chariot was a game-changing technology in other ways as well, arguably as significant as gunpowder would be later. The age of the chariot corresponds to the second millennium BCE waves of migrations and invasions of Indo-European speakers from northern and central Eurasia into the rimlands: the Hittites into Anatolia, Syria, and upper Mesopotamia; the Mycenaeans into the Greek peninsula; the so-called Aryans into Persia and India. The Hyksos, who were not Indo-European speakers, invaded Egypt with chariots around the same time. The chariot shows up suddenly, with no technological predecessors, in tombs from Shang China around 1200 BCE. Two centuries later, the Zhou, a people from the northwest with more access to horses, used massed chariots to overcome the Shang. Ancient elites across Eurasia, then, used chariots in military or symbolic ways: the Norse, Greco-Roman, Persian, and Indian gods all ride chariots.

The technical features of chariots and harness systems identified in archeological sites make it clear that these chariots across the continent share a common source. It is a case of diffusion that contributed to demographic shifts and political upheavals, helping to draw the map of the ancient world and permit the broad spread of Indo-European languages across the continent.

And yet, the chariot's day was relatively short. By the time of the Roman chariot races, or when chariots were buried with the first emperor of Qin or carved in relief in Han tombs, they were mere icons of power. Even when Homer described the chariot warfare on the plains of Troy, he was singing of warfare long obsolete. Chariots could be effectively challenged by infantry in hoplite formation, and proved no match for fast cavalry of mounted archers armed with the short compound bow. And with the invention and spread across Eurasia of the stirrup (from China, in the first centuries CE, with Indian and Kushani precedents), the archer sat all the more firmly in the saddle.

After the dissemination of the stirrup, the next highpoint of military technology transfer occurred, like so many other exchanges, during the Mongol period. To resolve a stalemated siege of southern Chinese cities in 1268, the Mongols brought in Persian siege engineers, who built versions of the European counterweight trebuchet (a kind of catapult) to bombard the cities. The Chinese called these "Muslim bombards," but to the Persian historian Rashid al-Din they were "Frankish" (that is, European) trebuchets. Such weapons had come to the Levant only decades before and had proved decisive at the Crusaders' siege of Acre in 1191.

Going the other way, at around the same time, was a momentous military technology: gunpowder and various kinds of guns. Gunpowder was a Chinese invention; an early formulation is described in a Daoist text from 850 CE. The early mixtures of sulfur and saltpeter with carboniferous substances (including honey) were, by the eleventh century, refined into powder that would explode, not just burn. Fireworks inspired various kinds of incendiary weapons (bombs, fire-arrows, rockets, and lances that spewed fire and potsherds), and ultimately by the thirteenth century exploding bombs in bamboo, then iron, casings. Song dynasty forces used these devices to defend their cities, for a time, against the Mongols. Smooth-bore cannons that could hurl projectiles were known from the late thirteenth and early fourteenth centuries in China.

The Mongols themselves did not make particular use of gunpowder weapons. Nevertheless, it is striking that knowledge about gunpowder and firearms took root in India, the Middle East, and Europe precisely during the Mongol era. It is likely that the information channels opened by the Mongol Empire helped spread this technology. The first field guns in Europe, from the early fifteenth century, closely resemble Chinese cannon of a century or so earlier. Again, the transfer of military technology is rapid.

Gunpowder and gunpowder weapons ultimately changed the way wars were fought; they also contributed to a common pattern of political consolidation across Eurasia, with centralization of power in monarchies including the Muscovites in Russia and Siberia, the Ottoman Empire, Safavids in Iran, the Mughals in India—states often dubbed "gunpowder empires"—as well as Tokugawa Japan and Ming China. In Europe, the arms race to create more powerful cannon, stronger fortifications, and more efficient firearm-wielding infantry put an end to feudalism and led to intense interstate competition and technological improvement in the manufacture and deployment of firearms. This in turn spurred the creation of overseas empires by the Spanish, Portuguese, Dutch, and ultimately Britain, France, and other European powers. It is not unreasonable to say that silk-road technology transfer in the Mongol era kick-started many military and political developments we associate with the early modern world.

Chapter 5
The arts on the silk road

While in Taiwan studying Chinese in the early 1980s, I turned on the TV one morning and happened upon a children's program. A young teacher was passing out juice boxes to her toddlers. Before they drank, however, she had them perform an experiment:

> "Xiao Zhang, can you bend a straw in half?"
> "I can! Look, teacher!"
> "Xiao Li, now try this: can you bend five straws all together?"
> "No, teacher, I can't!"
> "That's right. And what does this teach us, children?

"Unity is strength" was her answer. The lesson was certainly important for the Guomindang government of the Republic of China, living under the shadow of mainland China while trying to keep the lid on nativist Taiwanese opposition. But the story is universal. The image of the ancient fasces (bundled birch rods and axes) was already old when Rome adopted it as a symbol of state. In a tale attributed to Aesop ("The Bundle of Sticks"), a father teaches the same lesson to his sons. From there the story was much repeated across Eurasia. It shows up in *The Secret History of the Mongols*, the internal family chronicle of Genghis Khan's clan, where a female ancestor, Alan the Fair, uses a bundle of arrows to exhort her fractious sons to stick together. Tolstoy rewrote it in his collection of fables. Benito Mussolini borrowed the fasces to name his party—the Fascist Party—in 1922. The unbendable thirteen arrows bristle in the left talon of the eagle in the Great Seal of the United States, their bellicose symbolism balanced by an olive branch in the bird's right claw. And Caesar (the chimp) uses a handful of broken sticks to encourage simian solidarity in the 2011 remake of *Planet of the Apes*.

Silk-road stories

Such fables and motifs circulated for millennia across North Africa and Eurasia. As with other silk-road connections, Alexander's eastward conquest (fourth century BCE), likely played a role by bringing the Aesopian tradition to North India and Central Asia. Classical Greek writers refer to the existence of a book of Aesop's fables, just after Alexander's time, but it has not survived. There is no fixed Aesopian canon, and some even question whether the clever slave fabulist ever existed. What we now call Aesop's fables are the result of many interpolations over subsequent centuries, incorporating stories from other cultures and later times.

Indian folklore contributed to this body of Eurasian vernacular tales. Because of the long give-and-take between Hellenic and Indic tradition, it is usually impossible to establish Greek or Indian primacy for a given tale, but there are two written Indian sources that without doubt entered the mix—or reflect earlier Indian folklore that did so. The *Jākata*, a set of 547 folktales contained within the *Tripitika* (the three "baskets" of Buddhist scripture that Xuanzang later went to collect in India) is a collection of stories about the Buddha's past lives as man, god, or animal. These stories from the first millennium BCE are roughly contemporary with the Aesopian tradition and were assembled in the Buddhist canon in the fourth century and written down in the first century BCE. In one *Jākata* tale the Bodhisattva observes a jackal flattering a crow perched in a fruit tree. The crow, pleased, shakes some fruit down to the jackal. In the Aesopian version, "The Fox and the Crow," the crow has cheese in his mouth, which falls and is gobbled up by the fox when the bird opens his beak to respond to the fox's honeyed words. This version, written down in the first century CE in Greek and Latin, is well-known in modern Europe through Jean de la Fontaine's *Fables* and other retellings.

Other *Jākata* tales made their way to European literature through translations into Persian, Syriac, Arabic, and Hebrew, as well as Latin and Greek. For example, in two slightly varying *Jākata* tales, a Brahmin enlists a pair of parrots to spy and report on his adulterous wife while he is away from home on business. In the *Arabian Nights* version, after the parrot tells of the wife's transgressions, the wife successfully convinces her husband that the parrot is insane. She might have escaped her husband's wrath entirely but for a slave girl who tells on her. Some eighteen hundred years after this story was first collated in India, Chaucer's lusty Wife of Bath alluded to it, when, in defense of lying, she says in her Prologue that "a wise wife, if she knows what's for her good / Will swear the crow is mad, and in this mood / Call up for witness to it her own maid."

Jākata tales traveled eastward as well. The "Sumsumāra-jākata" tells of a female crocodile who wanted to eat the heart of a strapping young monkey (the Bodhisattva). Her crocodile mate promises to deliver the monkey to her and tries to trick the monkey by offering to ferry him to the opposite side of the Ganges, where tastier fruits grow. The monkey goes along, but when in mid-river the crocodile tries to drag him under the water so that the wife may eat his heart, the monkey explains that he has left his heart on top of a nearby fig tree. When the crocodile takes him to the bank to collect his heart, the monkey deftly escapes and ridicules the slow-witted predator from the tree's upper branches. This story was translated and adapted into Chinese in 251 CE by a Buddhist monk, Kang Senghui. In the early Chinese version, the crocodile is a turtle and the monkey's liver (the Chinese seat of the emotions) figures instead of his heart. Henceforth, Tibetan, Mongolian, Japanese, and Korean textual and folk versions appear, as well as

Chinese variants. In the Korean tale still told today, a turtle wants to deliver the liver to an ailing dragon in an undersea palace, and it is a rabbit, not a monkey, who outwits him. (As in the North American Br'er Rabbit stories—themselves distantly linked to the same Afro-Eurasian fabulary tradition—the Korean rabbit is a clever creature.)

Besides specific tales, certain genres and styles became common elements of Eurasian vernacular fiction. The *Jākata* tales, some religious, others with little obvious connection to Buddhist teaching, are bound together and given collective meaning when framed by introductory and concluding comments from the Buddha to his disciples. These pronounce a lesson and identify the Buddha's past lives as various other individuals. This frame-story structure is still more pronounced in the second influential Indian story collection, the *Panchatantra*. In this book, tales of beasts and assorted miscreant or exemplary humans (some overlapping with the *Jākata*) are framed as lessons for the instruction of princes. Within its five sections, there are stories within stories. This work was translated by 570 CE into literary Persian and in the eighth century into Arabic as *Kalilah wa Dimnah*. The Arabic translation became the source for translations into medieval European vernacular languages (from the eleventh century) as *The Fables of Bidpai*. The German version, *Das Buch der Beispiele* (1483), was one of the earliest works printed in Europe—a testament to the popularity of vernacular tales and the immediate commerciality of paper and printing. And the frame-story structure itself was widely imitated: in the *Arabian Nights* tradition, for example, nested stories are told nightly by Shahrzād to her murderous husband. In the fourteenth century Boccaccio's *Decameron* and, later, Chaucer's *Canterbury Tales* are structured similarly. Boccaccio's stories issue from the lovely mouths of ten noble young people escaping the Black Death in Florence to a country villa; Chaucer's earthier "sundry folk" tell their tales while on a pilgrimage.

A different aspect of the Indian folktale genre took root in China and possibly Japan and other parts of East Asia. Both *Jākata* tales and the *Panchatantra* are written in what is called prosimetric style—a mixture of prose and verse. The verse passages occur at key points in the narrative and might have been chanted or perhaps sung with musical accompaniment of drums and lutes, in a performance style that has continued up to modern times in South Asia. A cache of stories found in the library cave at Dunhuang seem to be a Chinese expression of this tradition. These stories are among the earliest examples of vernacular (as opposed to literary) written Chinese. Some have Buddhist themes, some are secular, but strikingly, unlike earlier Chinese fiction, they are written in the prosimetric style, which was without precedent in earlier Chinese literature. These vernacular narratives preserved at Dunhuang in Tang times, including story-elements from other parts of China as well as Indian and Central Asian lore, influenced the later development of Chinese drama (Yuan period) and vernacular fiction (Ming and Qing), both of which use alternating prose and verse.

Thus the traditions of medieval and early modern vernacular fiction in both Europe and East Asia blend indigenous folklore with genres, styles, and a reservoir of tales and motifs derived from India and the Helleno-Indic fusion of the first millennium BCE. This silk-road influence can be seen not only in collections of tales but also in the earliest novels or proto-novels east and west, including Murasaki Shikibu's *Tale of Genji* (early eleventh century), Cervantes's *Don Quixote* (early seventeenth century), and Cao Xueqin's *Dream of Red Mansions/Story of the Stone*, mid-eighteenth century).

Lutes

The most celebrated of Xinjiang's bazaars is in Kashgar. Today, like much of Kashgar's old city, the bazaar has been sanitized, organized, modernized, and harmonized into a dim echo of its former self, but not long ago you could buy apricots, saffron, tea, Bollywood-themed circumcision-party invitations, auto parts, farm tools, felted throw rugs, silk, and SIM cards all within a few yards of each other. A few steps on, and you could get your head shaved or teeth pulled. And just across the road you could buy live sheep or a horse.

A European or American tourist will on occasion test-drive a horse in the Kashgar livestock bazaar. It is striking to think that someone trained to ride in Arizona or Surrey can get on a horse in Xinjiang (or Mongolia or Kazakhstan), and both horse and rider know what to do. Although such horses are bred to be ridden, communication is not an instinctive outcome of the man-horse encounter. Rather, it is the result of culture, a set of signals learned by both parties, a body of knowledge trained into horse and human starting when that first domesticated stallion made his Faustian bargain to accept the rein in return for access to females. Despite differences in tack and riding styles, the fact that foreign riders can mount up and ride a Central Asian horse testifies to how equestrian culture has been shared around the globe over the past six thousand years.

A comparable phenomenon may be witnessed in another Kashgar institution: Muhemmet'emin Ababekri's stringed instrument shop in the old town. A first-time visitor there gapes at the display of gnarly lutes and viols hanging on the walls, with their almondine or melon-cap bodies, vestigial horns, protruding spikes, jangling rattles, oddly spaced frets, and strings by sevens and elevens, all resplendent in rococo pearlite inlay. Strange as they look, these instruments contain enough familiar chordophonic DNA that any Western porch-picker or garage-rocker can pick one up, figure out the tuning and fretting intervals, and pluck out a tune. That, like horsemanship, is the result of global dissemination of a Eurasian invention, in this case the lute and its offspring.

"Traditional" instrument ensembles of nearly all cultures across Eurasia and North Africa contain lutes. The earliest depictions of lutes—with long narrow necks and small bodies—are found in cylinder seal carvings from Akkadian Mesopotamia (2370–2110 BCE) and on a boundary stone from Susa (western Iran). The lutes are played by men, sometimes naked, often in proximity to wild animals. Are lutes, then, a Mesopotamian invention? Perhaps, but there may even be an earlier Central Asian nomadic connection, given the odd, possibly shamanistic iconography of the earliest lute images, the importance of animal materials (gut, hide, horsehair) in the manufacture of stringed instruments, and the fact that the later short-necked lute type, as well as the practice of playing with a bow, both come from Central Eurasia.

The Hyksos—chariot-riding nomad invaders—brought lutes to Egypt in the early second millennium, and these instruments appear in New Kingdom–era (1550–1070 BCE) paintings of banquets, but here in the hands of women as well as men. Greece had the lyre, a harplike instrument, from the second or first millennium BCE, but acquired lutes only much later, after Alexander's eastern conquests through Persia, Central Asia, and North India. The Greeks called their lute *pandoura*, a name that originates with the Sumerian word *pan-tur* ("bow-small"), which in turn gave us a long lineage of names for bowed instruments, plucked instruments, and drums: pandore, mandore, mandola, mandolin, vandola, bandurria, bandore, banjo, tanbur, tunbur, tunbura, tamboura, dombra, tambour, and tambourine.

Many of these lutes are recognizable close cousins: one set of "short-necked lutes" includes the Persian barbat, the western European lute, the Arabic oud ('ūd), various Indian lutes, the Chinese pipa, Korean pip'a, and Japanese biwa. This type of lute, with a pear-shaped body, rounded back, head-stock often set at an angle to the neck, and a shorter, sometimes fretted neck wide enough for multiple strings (and thus more harmonic possibilities) had a great impact across the silk road. Its earliest surviving representation is from a first-century BCE site of Kalchayan, Bactria, in what is now southern Uzbekistan. Other depictions show up in North Indian sculpture from the first century CE and Gandharan sculpture (Afghanistan) in the second to the fourth centuries.

It is likely that the short-necked barbat-type lute originated in Central Asia, or at least in the Hellenic-Kushani-Indian multicultural nexus. The Persian epic *Shahnamah* (Book of Kings) mentions the migration to Persia of 10,000 Lōris from Northern India, all "excelling in the art of the barbat."

The instrument thrived in Sasanid Persia (224–651 CE). A legend tells how Barbad, the most famous lutenist and musical theorist in the court of the Sasanid monarch Khosrow Parviz, used a barbat to convey the news of the death of the monarch's favorite horse. Bards in Kazakhstan and Kyrgyzstan tell a similar tale of informing a khan of his son's death through music on their own national lutes, the dombra and komuz, respectively. From Persia via Central Asia the barbat was brought to northern China by nomadic peoples (Xiongnu or Turks). The Chinese word "pipa" may even be derived from "barbat." Korean and Japanese versions of the instrument derived from Tang Chinese models.

The Arabs adopted the barbat from Persia around 600 CE and modified it, producing an instrument known as the oud, a fretless lute with a sound-box constructed of thin staves of wood instead of being carved from a single block (the Arabic word "'ūd" means "rod" or "stave"). The oud entered Moorish Spain and, later, Italy. In the thirteenth century the open-minded Holy Roman Emperor "Frederic of Sicily" (Frederic II, 1194–1250) brought it to Bavaria, in southern Germany, where a tradition of lute-making began that later migrated back to Italy and elsewhere. From Arabic "al-'ūd" derives the word "lute" in western European languages.

The oud/pipa became the preeminent instrument of its day in medieval times in both the Islamic world and China. Somewhat

7. Muslim and Christian play oud and lute in a thirteenth-century European manuscript. The short-necked lute probably originated in Afghanistan and from there spread to Persia as the barbat, to Arabia as the oud, and to China as the pipa.

later, despite its association with Muslim lands, it was crowned "queen of instruments" in Christian Europe through the fifteenth and sixteenth centuries. At the height of the Renaissance, any European of learning and means could be expected to play or at least own a lute—witness its frequent appearance in portraits and still lifes by Caravaggio, Titian, Vermeer, and other European painters. This Central Asian export out of Afghanistan, then, took on popularity and status akin to that enjoyed by the piano later as an instrument enjoyed both for entertainment and treasured by intellectuals on both ends of the continent. Why was that?

One reason may be the lute's design, on which it is easy to visualize variations in pitch: the strings along a fingerboard, with frets (or position markers where frets would be) crossing them at right angles, create a matrix that serves as a visual aid to understanding what happens acoustically when one shortens a string by pressing down at some point along its length. You cannot "see" sound changes with the voice or wind or percussion instruments: thus it is no accident that Pythagoras conducted his seminal musical experiments on a string, even though he took his initial inspiration from the sound of banging hammers. Only keyboard instruments (a later, European development) would provide an easier visual aid to musical investigation and theorizing than the lute.

Whatever the reason, the music of pipa ensembles became the primary court music of Tang China, particularly in the form of large suites (*daqu*), a set of dances in related keys, borrowed and adopted from Kucha, the Central Asian oasis in today's Xinjiang. Modes and scales of this music, realized on the pipa, developed into the Tang theory of eighty-four musical modes. The suites, theory, and pipa itself were adopted as a fixed form in Japan, and even in modern times the Japanese *tōgaku* (Tang music) echoes the timbres and modes of the medieval silk road.

In Europe, lutes were not such an exponent for music theory, although they did become a primary instrument for playing art music. From around the year 1500 players started to play with the fingers of their right hands, rather than plucking single notes with a pick or quill. This technique, together with extra strings added to the lute, allowed lutenists to play complex polyphony (harmony and counterpoint), making the lute a virtuosic solo instrument as well as an accompaniment for singers. It was central, along with organs, clavichords, and other emerging keyboard instruments, to the revolution in harmonic complexity in European music.

It was in the Islamic world, however, where the lute played its most important theoretical role. Islamic musical theorists—who were also philosophers and scientists—faced a challenge reconciling the largely theoretical musicology inherited from Greek sources (including Pythagoras, Aristotle, Euclid, and Ptolemy), which were seen as ideal, with actual music as sung and played in their own parts of the Arabic-, Persian-, and Turkic-speaking world. The main issues began with temperament—how discrete notes are defined from the infinite possibilities in the continuous frequency spectrum—and from there to the definitions of scales (linear sets of notes), of intervals (distances between notes), and of modes (groups of notes with certain melodic qualities and emotive associations). In part it was a mathematical problem, which the Islamic Golden Age polymaths al-Kindi, al-Farabi, and Ibn Sini (Avicenna) rendered concrete by mapping note values as fingerings on the neck of the lute. Zalzal and Ishaq al-Mawsili, musicians untrained in Greek science, likewise used the lute itself to discuss and defend the sound of indigenous music against Hellenic theory.

As an example of what these musical differences entailed, consider the "happy-sounding" major triad, defined by its major third (C–E–G); and now the "sad-sounding" minor triad, with a minor third (C–E♭–G). But what if you played a note with a frequency precisely *between* the major and minor thirds, in this example, between the E and E♭? You can't do this on the modern piano, but you could on the fretless oud (and other fretless stringed instruments) by placing the left-hand finger at a position between those for major and minor thirds. In fact, this note is called *"wusta Zalzal"* (Zalzal's second-finger fret) after the neutral third characteristic of Arabic and Persian music, a note not found in Greek or later European music. Al-Farabi and others reconciled Hellenic theory with Islamic musical practice by allowing for such quarter-tones and other microtones.

Such analysis resulted in an approach to categorizing music used across the Islamic silk road. The modal system is known as *dastgah* in Persian, and most commonly by versions of the Arabic word *muqam*, meaning "position," or "place." (*Raga* in South Asia are similarly organized, and overlap to a degree with muqam; the sitar is a fretted long-necked lute—but the frets are designed to be movable, precisely to accommodate different note values of various ragas, or modes.), and overlap to a degree with muqam. Different cultures feature their own sets of muqam pieces or suites, each in theory defined by musical modes, though in practice they have strayed from strict theory and adopted rhythms, dances, lyrics, and other local characteristics as defining features. Some groups of muqams are linked to specific ethnic groups or regions. In nation-states of the former Soviet Union, the regional muqams have been transcribed and their texts fixed by state committees, publishing houses, and arts academies, and promoted as the national music. Azerbaijanis are proud that more than two minutes of their *mugham* comprise a track on the Golden Record, a twelve-inch analog disk launched in 1977 on the *Voyager* spacecraft toward the edge of the solar system. The Uzbeks and Tajiks each codified their own separate versions of *Shashmaqom* ("Six Muqams") under the influence of Soviet nationalizing policies—though they both derived from the same Central Asian tradition. The Peoples Republic of China officially promotes the Twelve Muqams of the Uyghurs as a "Chinese" folk-music form while de-emphasizing its place in the Islamic muqam tradition. That notwithstanding, Uyghurs are no less proud of their muqams, which the PRC efforts have gained a place on the UNESCO Representative List of the Intangible Cultural Heritage of Humanity.

Visual arts

There are myriad examples of painting, carving, architecture, textiles, ceramics, and other two- and three-dimensional physical artifacts that demonstrate silk-road contacts and exchanges. They also illuminate the nature of those interactions. If we find Chinese bronze mirrors in Ferghana, Chinese-made textiles in a tomb in Egypt, or Chinese ceramics in a palace in Istanbul, we know that someone carried them there by caravan or ship. But what about a Sasanian-style silver platter found near Xi'an, the old Tang capital of Chang'an, with both Persian and Chinese elements in it? Or the massive fountain bar at Karakorum, made by a French silversmith for the Mongol court? In these cases, the objects are locally made, perhaps by craftsmen who themselves came from far away. The Mongols in particular loved to transport specialists around, gathering them in their eastern capital or exchanging them between courts in China and Iran. Before the Mongols there were Soghdians, Turks, and other foreigners in China, and Chinese captives in Samarkand or even Baghdad, many with special artistic skills.

So, objects moved and makers of objects moved. Yet a third mechanism of exchange involves just an idea moving, the "stimulus diffusion" when a motif, design, style, or technology from one place was observed and imitated by other artists and craftsmen elsewhere. Sasanian birds, animals, and mythical creatures decorate textiles that are otherwise fully Byzantine. Hellenic or Iranian motifs show up in Han or Tang Chinese metal work or ceramics. Chinese designs often traveled westward on textiles, only to be realized in tiles, painting, or other media in the Islamic lands or Europe.

Finally, there are full hybrids no longer identifiable as one regional tradition or another but comprising mixed traditions or joint efforts, such as the Indic, Iranian, and Hellenic fusion found in Buddhistic statuary under the Kushan empire in Gandhara. Such hybrids comprise new, eclectic traditions in their own right.

Once such complicated case of diffusion would be the halo. Its appearance in Buddhist and, a little later, Christian iconography, and even in Mughal book illuminations suggests a Eurasian connection, which scholars say arises from a common source in the Iranian tradition. Both the Iranian god Mithra and the prophet Zoroaster were given either plain or "radiate" halos (with sunbeams) as an attribute suggesting divinity and power. Earlier

8. A second-century CE Gandharan frieze of the Buddha and Vajrapani / Heracles. The Buddha's robes and the toga on Heracles are rendered in the Hellenic style. The Buddha has a halo; his guardian holds a club—a Mediterranean motif associated with the hero Heracles—and a thunderbolt (*vajra*)—an attribute of the bodhisattva Vajrapani.

still, Scythian, Bactrian, and Kushani kings on coins from the first century BCE are depicted with halos. A ring found in the Issyk Kurgan tomb in Kazakhstan of the Saka (Scythian) noble known as Golden Man bears an image of a head with a full radiate halo. This dates from the fourth–third century BCE. Roman emperors and Christ are first depicted with halos starting eight hundred years later, from the time of Constantine in the fourth century CE. The diffusion of the halo from Indo-European speakers on the Eurasian steppes to painters and carvers of Christian and Buddhist figures at either end of the continent thus involved more than just the movement of objects or craftsmen: it was an idea, transmitted long distances over a long period of time, no doubt through a combination of objects transported and humans moving.

The "Three Hares" is a more whimsical—and still more mysterious—example of the complex transmission of a motif. At the apex of ceilings in at least sixteen of the Mogao cave temples at Dunhuang, dating from the Sui (581–618 CE) and Tang (618–906 CE) dynasties, are roundels depicting three rabbits or hares chasing each other in a circle. The creatures share ears, so that where there should be six, there are only three ears, together forming a triangle. The Dunhuang versions of this motif are the earliest, but it shows up again (sometimes with four linked rabbits) in temples in Tibet (tenth–seventeenth centuries) and Ladakh (twelfth–thirteenth centuries), on an Iranian tray and coin (thirteenth century), on a reliquary casket decorated with Arabic calligraphy and found in southern Russia (thirteenth–fourteenth century), and as ceiling bosses and other decorations in thirteenth–fifteenth-century cathedrals and churches in France, Germany, Switzerland, and Britain, with some nineteenth-century copies. There are nineteen medieval carvings of the three rabbits in Devon, England, alone.

From the chronology of the diffusion, it seems that the Three Hares motif traveled during the Mongol period. It generally shows up in religious architectural contexts, but no one knows exactly

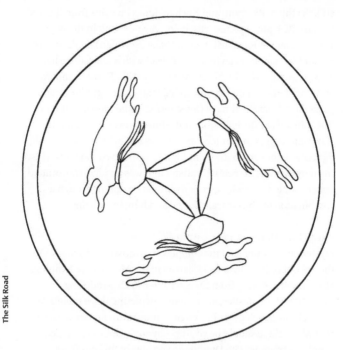

9. The "three hares" motif, here from the ceiling of cave 407 at Dunhuang, China (ca. 589–618). This enigmatic trompe l'oeil image spread across Eurasia in the thirteenth century, and versions are found in South Asia, Persia, Russia, and western Europe.

what it means. The motif may have been transmitted on textiles—yet it shows up in England on ceilings just as it does on the Central Asian frontier of China. Like the halo, then, the three-rabbits motif involved long-term, long-distance conveyance of an idea, perhaps even a rise to international fashionablity, in a manner we can no longer recapture.

The best examples of direct artistic influence and cross-fertilization across the silk road are found in Islamic book illuminations from the fourteenth century, a style of painting known as the Persian miniature. There had been illustrations in earlier Arabic and Persian books, especially scientific manuscripts, but also in *Kalilah wa Dimnah*, the Arabic translation of the *Panchatantra*. The narrative style of book painting took off following the Mongol conquests and reached a peak in the various courts of Timur's successors (of which the Mughals in India were one). Islam disapproves of representations of human forms; although this meant that there were few murals or large-scale paintings after the rise of Islam, it did not preclude vivid narrative portrayals, within the private pages of books and albums, of episodes from such works as Ferdowsi's *Shahnamah* (Book of Kings), Nizami's *Khamza*, or to illustrate Hafiz's poetry. The favorite themes were drawn from pre-Islamic literature, including the love story of Khosrow and Shirin, adventures of the warrior Rustam and hunter Bayram Gur, and the mythologized exploits of Iskandar (Alexander), but miniatures could also depict stories from the life of the prophet Muhammad, or scenes of contemporary rulers picnicking, hunting, or in battle.

The most important centers of the miniaturist art were Tabriz, Baghdad, Shiraz, and Herat, but skillful calligraphers, gilders, and bookbinders as well as painters worked in academies across the Eurasian Islamic world. Miniaturist painting was a multinational artistic form—and thus we speak of Mughal miniatures, Ottoman (or Turkish) miniatures, Mamluk miniatures, and so on, each with their own characteristics and paths of development—including the absorption of European influence. Nobel Prize–winner Orhan Pamuk's 1998 novel, *My Name Is Red*, concerns the sixteenth-century milieu of book artists in Istanbul, though their world extends even beyond the boundaries of Ottoman lands. As the story begins, the miniaturist Kara (Black) has just returned from twelve years in Persia.

One striking feature of miniatures, especially those from fourteenth- to sixteenth-century Central Asia and Iran, is their Chinese influence, which arose from the Mongol penchant for moving artists and artworks between courts in China and the Middle East. In these paintings clouds often take classic Chinese *ruyi* form—mimicking the shape of the auspicious *lingzhi* mushroom. Echoes of Chinese landscape painting are likewise evident in the delineation of mountains and rocky outcroppings, with their heavy shading of serried ledges, as well as in the ways that trees, flowers, and fire are drawn, not to mention the occasional appearance of a dragon or phoenix.

How was this influence conveyed? There were Chinese artists in the Il-Khanid capitals of Maraga and Tabriz, but Muslim artists also took inspiration from portable objects: Chinese ceramics, drawing primers, scroll paintings, and textiles, all of which were available to the Il-Khanids as well as in Samarkand, Herat, and other Timurid capitals. A look at a Persian miniature, then, can be a glimpse into the history of the silk road, especially its Mongol and Timurid floruit. They demonstrate the cultural integration of the Islamic world, as well as the links to China forged by the Mongols and Timurids.

Blue-and-white ware

Think of "a Chinese vase." Your mind's eye almost certainly envisions a delicate white porcelain with a blue pattern: a style known in Chinese as *qinghua ci*, or blue flower ware. For many of us, this genre epitomizes Chinese porcelain; it is in fact another case of continental cross-fertilization. The pigment that produces the intense blue in ceramics was first used farther west; the earliest examples show up in ancient Egyptian artifacts, and there are examples of Islamic blue-and-white ware from the ninth to the eleventh centuries. But starting in the ninth century, cobalt mined in Persia was exported to Tang China, where it was known as "Muslim blue." The 830 CE Belitung shipwreck in Indonesian waters contains the only known examples of Tang blue-and-white ware, which use cobalt blue pigment, but here the cobalt is painted on a white slip over pottery, not directly on translucent white

10. The Simurgh, a mythical, benevolent flying creature, rescues the infant Zal in a detail of a late-sixteenth-century miniature from Safavid Iran. Zal, a foundling born with snow-white hair, later founds the race of kings who are the subject of the epic *Shanamah*. Chinese influence is evident in the portrayal of the rocks, clouds, and the sinuous flowering tree in the center of the crag. After the Mongol era, depictions of this mythical bird resemble the Chinese *fenghuang*, or phoenix.

kaolin porcelain. The ship itself, an Arab dhow, was plying the maritime silk road from China en route to Africa when it sank.

The blue-and-white china we know today arose during the Yuan (1279–1368) and subsequent Ming (1368–1644) dynasties. Increased imports of Persian cobalt, made possible thanks to Mongol imperial communications, combined with breakthroughs in ceramic technology. In the southern Chinese town of Jingdezhen, potters learned to paint or stencil designs not on a slip, as on the Tang pottery, but directly onto the dried white kaolin clay under a clear glaze, and then fire it at extremely high temperature. The result was *qinghua ci*.

Jingdezhen blue-and-white ware developed under Chinese court patronage, particularly that of the Mongol Yuan, but it increasingly became an export product. Many Chinese literati in the Ming actually considered blue-and-white ware foreign and vulgar. Islamic courts in Central, South, and Southwest Asia, on the other hand, valued Chinese blue-and-white highly. The Safavid shah Abbas I (r. 1588–1629) is said to have imported Chinese potters and Ming wares, and the Ottomans' Topkapi Palace collection holds 10,358 pieces of Chinese blue-and-white dating from the Yuan to the Qing dynasties. Chinese artisans produced pieces specifically for the Islamic market, with Islamic geometric motifs and calligraphy in Arabic and Persian.

Blue-and-white ware was also frequently imitated along the silk road. For example, from the fifteenth century potters in Iznik, in western Anatolia, made their own version of Chinese blue-and-white by copying pieces taken by the Ottomans as loot from Tabriz, Damascus, and Cairo. They did not use porcelain but overlaid a red clay ware with a white slip decorated with such Chinese motifs as dragons, phoenixes, lotuses, and peonies. In addition to the blue-and-white palate, Iznik artisans later added polychrome expressions of fruit and flowers, especially tulips. Their elaborately painted tiles decorated the interiors of Istanbul's mosques—hence the nickname the "Blue Mosque" of the Sultan Ahmed Mosque (1616). Iznik decoration, while inspired by Chinese ceramics, developed its own vocabulary influenced by calligraphy and decorative motifs from architecture, carpets, book illumination, and locally cultivated flowers. Needless to say, such fine freehand work designed for imperial mosques and sultans' palaces was extremely expensive. Surviving documents tell us that a single tile sold for more than five times the daily wage of a skilled craftsman, with tableware even more costly.

Starting in the sixteenth century, Jingdezhen also exported china to Europe, first via Southeast Asia. Later the Portuguese, who imported 40,000 to 60,000 pieces by the 1520s, and the Dutch, who named their blue-and-white pottery *kraak* ware after the Portuguese carrack ships that carried it, purchased their wares from China directly. European tin-glazed imitations soon appeared, and before the end of the sixteenth century native potters in Puebla, west of Mexico City, were making blue-and-white ware under the supervision of Spanish monks. Such was the European craze for blue-and-white ware that when the Jingdezhen kilns were shut down for a decade during a late-seventeenth century rebellion against the Manchu conquerors in China, the Dutch ordered imitation blue-and-white from Safavid Persia. This "Kubachi" ware (named for the Caucasus town where much of this type of pottery was found) came complete with decorations of pagodas and hills.

The Dutch were hooked on *kraak*. In 1636, vessels of the Dutch East India company (VOC) shipped 259,000 pieces from its base in Batavia (Jakarta). From these models, Holland's blue-and-white-ware industry took root in the former breweries of Delft, whose now-prized dishes and tiles were initially simple imitations dominated by Chinese motifs. Italy, France, and Germany all produced their own versions of blue-and-white. But it was the new English ceramics industry in the eighteenth and nineteenth centuries whose mass production techniques in

11. Two blue-and-white dishes with grape decoration, at top a fifteenth-century porcelain from Chinese kilns at Jingdezhen, at bottom a sixteenth-century stone-paste dish from Ottoman Iznik. Although Iznik blue-and-white imitates Ming *qinghua ci*, the grape motif itself was imported to China from Sasanian Persia and still held foreign associations in Ming times.

stoneware and paste porcelain brought Chinoiserie blue-and-white to tables everywhere. The bucolic "willow-pattern" design, with its houseboats, peaked bridges, soaring swallows, pagodas, and pavilions with up-turned eaves, took the aesthetic preferences of khans and sultans to the level of high kitsch, giving many of us our first sense of what china (and China) looked like. At a time when very few Americans or Europeans could use chopsticks, some supermarkets in the United States in the 1960s and 1970s gave away a piece of industrial blue-and-white willow-pattern tableware each week to loyal shoppers. The Chinese were not the first to make money knocking off luxury goods.

Chapter 6
Whither the silk road?

It is a staple of world history textbooks that the silk road reached an unprecedented height of activity during the *pax Mongolica*, only to decline thereafter, its emporia shuttered, its unfrequented lanes blown over by the sands of time. Central Eurasia, it is said, remained mired in the slough of despond until European colonization and excavation reopened it to modernity. What delivered this death blow to the silk road, we are told, was the advent of direct maritime trade from Western Europe: carracks and galleons, Vasco da Gama and his Spanish, Dutch, and English successors at their helms, displacing the caravans of anonymous Orientals. The argument is implicitly economic: it being cheaper to haul goods by sea, overland trade could not compete with maritime trade. The year 1500 is thus a very convenient and satisfying dividing point: running before the wind, valiant seaborne explorers sail into the dawn of a new era, volume 1 ends, you can pick up volume 2 at the campus bookstore, see you next semester.

Why the silk road never died

But the reports of the silk road's early modern demise are greatly exaggerated. For one thing, while western European merchant ships were newly arrived in East Asian waters in the sixteenth century, maritime trade routes had for centuries already linked

China to the Indian Ocean, the east African coast, and even via the Persian Gulf to the Mediterranean. As the ninth-century Belitung shipwreck shows, quantities of china had been moving west by ship during one of the overland silk road's most active moments—so maritime competition was neither new nor debilitating to transcontinental exchange but complementary. More to the point, the silk road was not only about trade in goods but also about the movement of ideas. While it was certainly cheaper to transport heavy items like ceramics from southern China by sea, ceramic technology and decorative motifs moved overland just as easily, along with textiles, copybooks, and the artisans themselves. Jingdezhen wares likely came to Istanbul's Topkapi Palace by sea, but the locally made Iznik blue-and-whites are there thanks to a long-term overland interaction.

Such debates turn to a certain extent on how one defines the term "silk road" and what aspect one chooses to focus on. But even looking simply at the empirical evidence of the most famous silk-road phenomena—dissemination of religion and movement of goods—we find significant exchanges through the sixteenth, seventeenth, and eighteenth centuries, the era when received wisdom claims that the silk road was dead. Sufi orders were especially active in Central Eurasia throughout this period, proselytizing among the nomad tribes left disaggregated after the collapse of Mongol and Timurid imperial unifications. The Naqshibandiyya order, in particular, made great inroads into Xinjiang, northeast Tibet, and western China, expanding numbers of adherents and shaping the character of Islamic practice there.

The Ming dynasty had no direct military presence in Central Asia—unlike the Han, Tang, or Mongol dynasties before it—and for this reason some scholars have argued that Ming China was isolated and the silk road moribund. Timurid princes and rump Mongol rulers in Central Asia were indeed a fractious lot, and with no imperial overlord to secure the routes, trade was hazardous. But Mirza Muhammad Haidar, a Central Asian historian, wrote in

Persian in the mid-sixteenth century that a peace deal concluded by two Chaghatayid brothers in Xinjiang had "resulted [in] such security and prosperity for the people, that any one might travel alone between Kamul [Hami] or Khitai [China] and the country of Farghana without provision for the journey and without fear of molestation." In 1558 the Englishman Anthony Jenkinson observed in Bukhara that the caravans from China had been interrupted by wars for three years, but that usually "from the countries of Cathay are brought thither in time of peace, and when the way is open, musk, rhubarb, satin, damask, with divers other things." The Jesuit laybrother Bento de Goes—like Xuanzang or the Sufis, another religious specialist on the road—traveled from Kabul to western China in 1603–4, joining a merchant's caravan in Yarkand. In fact, Ming dynasty annals report frequent embassies from Central Asia and the Middle East during the dynasty's first centuries, and even after these tapered off somewhat between 1544 and the end of the dynasty in 1644, seventy official missions licensed by western princes arrived in Beijing. Each of the nearly annual missions brought tribute goods and dozens of Central Asian merchants to Beijing.

As Russia expanded from the mid-sixteenth century into the power vacuum left in Siberia by the disintegration of the Mongol Golden Horde, it opened trade relations with India and China. From India, Russians sought colorful cotton textiles. Because the Mughals and other polities in north India needed to replenish their supplies of horses annually, they traded cotton piece goods and indigo and other dyes for hundreds of thousands of Central Asian horses. This trade was worth more annually, according to one historian's calculation, than that of the English and Dutch East India Companies' Bengal exports combined. Central Asian merchants in turn exchanged the Indian goods with Russians. This was an exchange of textiles for horses, brokered by Central Asian middlemen: the epitome of silk-road trade. From China, moreover, Russia began trading furs for tea and rhubarb (not the rhubarb stalks we eat in pies, but the roots of a breed found in the foothills of Tibet and highly valued in Europe as an astringent and purgative). If the silk road had disappeared, why was there so much trade along it?

Meanwhile, the Manchu power that founded the new Qing dynasty in China conquered Mongolia and Xinjiang by the mid-eighteenth century. The trade routes thus secured, Chinese merchants and the Qing state shipped Chinese products to the borders, whence nomads and merchants from Central Asian oases reshipped them farther west—again in a pattern of conquest followed by trade dating back to at least the first century BCE. Kazakh taste was even able to influence Chinese manufacturing through the mid-nineteenth century: the Qing archives contain hundreds of what are in effect market research reports on Kazakh preferences for silks. These nomads favored everyday satin, damask, and pongee over more costly brocades and dragon robes, and while they loved crimson, iridescent green, indigo, moon-white, purple, and granary grey, they would not trade their sheep and horses for satins in pink, peach, watery red, or light green. The factories in southeast China, thousands of miles away, responded with alacrity to consumer demand signals and altered production accordingly, just as they do today when global fashions for blue jeans, handbags, or running shoes change.

Still, although the silk road did not die by the sixteenth century, as some historians have asserted, big changes in Eurasia nonetheless reshaped its underpinnings forever. The first of these was geopolitical. Russian and Qing expansion enclosed the steppe in a way that put an end to the independent Inner Eurasian nomad state. Significantly, both Russian and Qing states had inherited elements of the Mongol imperial heritage, but what made possible their territorial expansion and consolidation of control over Central Eurasia was their superior communications and logistical capabilities, backed by the wealth of their large agrarian regions. By the nineteenth century, modern firearms and military drill also played an important role for the Russians. Thus agrarian Russia and China, formerly under the Tartar boot, turned the tables on the nomads and met each other in the middle of the continent. Their later avatars, the USSR and PRC, inherited the spoils.

The second change was technological. Industrialization, in particular mankind's unleashing of energy stored in fossil fuels, downgraded the importance of animal power for both war and commerce across Eurasia. This did not happen overnight: donkey carts still outnumbered motor vehicles as taxis in Kashgar in 1990. But the transition to hydrocarbons has been ineluctable, and the donkey carts are mostly gone now. This technological shift undermined both the steppe peoples' military edge and their economic comparative advantage (raising horses). Central Asia lost the geopolitical centrality it had enjoyed since equine domestication.

New technology also rewrote the rules of trade. Under the premodern energy regime, to transport goods economically even for medium-range regional trade—let alone across the continent—those goods had to be of high value relative to their weight. Maritime trade was cheaper, but even so it was limited by size of the vessels, seasonality of winds, and the hazards of sea voyages. Thus silk-road goods, whether moved by land or by sea, were expensive luxuries: medicines, spices, rare animals and birds, works of art, rich textiles, precious metals and gems, skilled humans (artisans, musicians, dancing girls, holy men).

Today, however, while we still trade luxuries globally (wine from Bordeaux to China, Chinese-manufactured iPhones to the United States) we also ship around the world commodities worth only pennies a pound, such as soybeans, wheat, oil, cotton, or scrap metal. Perhaps the best example of the new calculus governing long-distance trade is the Jiulong Company founded by Zhang Yin. Zhang exports scrap paper from the United States as backhaul in container ships that, after delivering Chinese products to U.S. consumers, would otherwise sail largely empty on their return trip (since the United States exports few manufactures to China). In her Guangdong factory Zhang Yin recycles the American waste paper into packaging materials, which she sells to Coca-Cola, Nike, Sony, Haier, and other firms. After 1985 Zhang quickly became China's richest woman simply by importing and reprocessing what Americans throw out with the trash. Paper, the ancient silk-road product, remains relevant; but it is fossil fuels that make it again eligible for long-distance trade.

In postindustrial times, then, there has been global trade and Eurasian trade, but we might be hard-pressed to call it silk-road trade. Likewise, the Central Eurasian states have ceded their geopolitical significance to countries along the Eurasian rim. If not by the sixteenth century, then, would we declare the silk road deceased by the nineteenth or twentieth?

Consider this case: a country on one end of Eurasia promotes a religious system through military, political, and diplomatic means. A country on the other end, attracted by the religious system, studies it eagerly, translating its textual corpus. Envoys pass back and forth. Besides the religion itself, however, much else is titrated from one country and civilization to another, including technology, music, and art. One country imitates the artistic styles of the other, carving similar statuary and erecting its temples and palaces in a related architectural style.

This could describe the long relationship between India and China, revolving around Buddhism. But it could also describe the shorter-lived, more intense contact between the Soviet Union and the People's Republic of China during the 1950s—with Marxism-Leninism in the role of "religion." The decade of Sino-Soviet cooperation saw Chinese studying Russian in schools; Soviet technical personnel went to China to set up factories and advise on a range of political and security matters, including nuclear technology. Not only does China's political system reflect the Soviet Leninist model (imitation that began with the founding of the Chinese Communist Party in 1921), but Russian influence through the twentieth century also left a mark in film, literature, and music—even such things as the popularity of the accordion. One can still see visual evidence of this latter day "silk road" exchange in the architecture of China's cities, just as in Eastern Europe, Central Asia, and Mongolia. From the middle of Tian'anmen Square in Beijing, turn around 360 degrees: besides the gate to the Qing dynasty palace, with its Mao portrait, the eye takes in the bulky Stalinist neoclassical architecture of the Great Hall of the People to the west and the National Museum of China on the east. On the bas relief on the plinth of the Monument to the People's Heroes, buff men and buxom women strike the triumphant poses favored in Soviet socialist realist art. This style characterizes virtually all official public statuary from the PRC's first five decades—including even the dancing grape girls in downtown Turfan—as well as many propaganda posters and mid-century oil painting. And the Mao mausoleum behind the monument affords Communist China's first leader the same mummified immortality enjoyed by Lenin, the Bulgarian leader Georgi Dimitrov, Khorloogiin Choibalsan of Mongolia, Stalin (until 1961), Klement Gottwald of Czechoslovakia, Ho Chi Minh of Vietnam, Kim Il-sung and now Kim Jong-il of North Korea, Agostinho Neto of Angola, and Forbes Burnham of Guyana.

One of the most significant, but seldom noticed, examples of Soviet influence in China is in urban domestic architecture—the ubiquitous apartment towers built for decades to accommodate the swelling populations of China's cities. While in many ways similar to low-rent projects or council-house flats found in the United States or Britain, the entries to these apartments were designed to facilitate the social control important to both Soviet and PRC regimes. Groups of buildings were often arranged and numbered in small districts (*mikroraĭon* in Russian, *qu* in Chinese). Each building had multiple numbered entryways (*podezd*/*danyuan*), which led upwards by stairs and/or elevators to landings upon which a few apartments open. In Socialist days, light bulbs in these stairways were notoriously missing or broken. Residents of these vertically subdivided units had to enter and exit via a single entryway and reach their apartments by the same elevator or stairway. In Soviet Russia, a formidable *babushka* would preside over the entryway from the ground floor; in nicer apartment buildings, such a woman kept an eye on the elevator and was known as *liftersha*. In China, invigilation of residents was likewise the job of older women, who often made their "offices" in the elevator. They would decorate the walls, bring in a heater, and push the elevator buttons with a long stick while seated on a stool. As a legacy of Soviet influence, similar buildings may also be found across Eurasia, in both Poland and Mongolia, for example.

The "Eurasianist" school of Russian historiography has been fascinated by Russia's position abutting Asia and its long contact with steppe peoples. Some have argued that the authoritarianism that overtook socialism under Russian (and Chinese) stewardship is a kind of eastern deviation, a Tartar infection that distorted Marx's philosophy, wrenching it off course onto a path that purely European socialists would not have taken. This argument is simply another reiteration of the environmental determinist theories and the "Oriental despot" stereotype we saw in Ammianus Marcellinus, Gibbon, or *Mulan*. But there are real parallels between pan-Eurasian exchanges during the Soviet era and earlier epochs of imperial unification, when material goods and personnel circulated across the continent in concert with the dissemination of an ideological system. China adopted Soviet-style apartment buildings in the twentieth century under circumstances similar to those when it adopted the chair (and much else) from India in the tenth and eleventh centuries. If we look at silk-road phenomena broadly, we can see quantitative difference but little qualitative difference between the exchange of goods and ideas across Eurasia from prehistoric to early modern times and what we now speak of as "globalization." As an aspect of human history, the silk road never died; it simply extended to ever-broader horizons.

Modern echoes

The historical resonances of the term "silk road" remain potent in many areas. In international relations, "silk road" is shorthand for bilateral or multilateral relations across a region including China, Central Asia, South Asia, Iran, Turkey, and Russia. In July 2011, U.S. Secretary of State Hillary Clinton delivered a foreign policy speech in Chennai, India, in which she pointed out that "historically, the nations of South and Central Asia were connected to each other and the rest of the continent by a sprawling trading network called the Silk Road." Marc Grossman, the U.S. Special Representative for Afghanistan and Pakistan, repeated the message in Islamabad, Pakistan, a few weeks later. The United States thus branded its efforts to enhance India's influence, spur economic integration in the region, smooth border-crossing for goods and people, ease India-Pakistan tensions, and help with Afghanistan's development, with a slogan based on historical imagination: "Let's work together to create a new Silk Road."

Of course, Clinton's north–south corridor of "South and Central Asia" no doubt intentionally left out key silk-road participants to the immediate west and east. Yet these players, too, eagerly embrace the silk-road image. On the occasion of the fortieth anniversary of diplomatic ties between Iran and China, Iran's foreign minister, Ali Akbar Salehi, noted that "the Islamic Republic of Iran and the People's Republic of China are two civilized countries and enjoy an ancient history, and the silk road, which has worldwide fame, is considered the historical symbol of relations between the two nations." This diplomatic boilerplate accurately highlights the antiquity and foundational nature of both Persian and Sinic civilizations, a key aspect of both countries' self-identity that has often been neglected by western diplomatic discourse in its more imperious moments. Not to be outdone, Pakistan's president Asif Ali Zardari resorted to the silk-road metaphor himself. Following an attack on a restaurant in 2011 by a group of Uyghur militants active in Kashgar, China announced that the militants had been trained in Pakistan. Speaking at an international trade fair in Urumchi soon after these attacks, President Zardari promised cooperation and pledged that "the Silk Road will be fully revived." And later that year, the quasi-official Chinese tabloid *Global Times* (*Huanqiu shibao*) responded to a U.S. diplomatic outreach to Burma and to the American "New Silk Road Strategy" with an editorial advising that China should "Revive the silk road, smash American containment."

But anyone, not just diplomats, can cash in on the silk road's romantic appeal. Almost any Eurasian city, from Ningbo to Tbilisi to Istanbul to Venice can be called an "ancient silk road city." Travel companies market trips under the name—but read the fine print, because while a "silk road tour" will most likely take you to China, you could end up in Central Asia, Iran, Nepal, Turkey, or even the North Caucasus. Restaurateurs love the silk-road concept: there are restaurants called "Silk Road" serving Uyghur food in Beijing, Shanghai, Toronto, Etobicoke, Sydney, Adelaide, Oakleigh, and London. But a silk-road restaurant need have little to do with Central Asia: "Silk road" is to "Asian fusion" in the twenty-first century what the Tiki bar was to "Chinese-Polynesian" food in the mid-twentieth. A place in the posh Georgetown area of Washington, DC, serves "Silk Road–inspired Regional American Cuisine" in "a colorful Moroccan Bazaar, exotic Tibetan Lounge . . . a Turkish Tent and a classic English bar dramatically influenced by Hong Kong's international cutting edge allure." There's a Silk Road restaurant in Missoula, Montana, offering tapas; a Silk Road in Walnut Creek, California, just voted "best Greek" restaurant, and a "Silk Road Café" in an Irish castle with what's been called the best Middle Eastern/North African cuisine in Dublin.

In music and dance, the notion of the silk road often suggests the kind of Sino-Islamic mash-up that inspired Puccini's *Turandot*, but the musical and choreographic origins of "silk-road music" could derive from anywhere in the Old World. Yo-Yo Ma's Silk Road Ensemble commissions and performs colorful hybridic works from across Eurasia. However, an earlier, and possibly the first, musician to commercially assume the silk-road mantle was Kitaro, whose "Silk Road" synthesizer compositions arguably founded the genre of New Age music. Kitaro provided the background music for the long-running *Silk Road* documentary series, produced by NHK, Japanese national public television, but I remember it best pumped from speakers at an outdoor hot-tub place in Santa Cruz, just a few yards from an old school bus repainted with purple lotuses.

For the 2011 autumn/winter season, while Giorgio Armani took inspiration from "the Far East," Oscar de la Renta looked to "the Silk Road," and rolled out a "magic carpet ride" complete with "ottoman jackets . . . embroidered in the manner of Bukhara carpets," "jewel-like costumes of the court of Tz'u-hsi . . . 'Dragon Empress' of China," "North African threadwork . . . patchwork paisley tunics," "ostrich feather skirts," and "gigantic 'Genghis Khan' fox hats." No doubt, such outfits could be well complemented by Le Métier de Beauté's 2011 fall/winter collection "Introducing Silk Road, a journey of discovery and luxurious sensuality." The Silk Road Kaleidoscope eye-shadow palate features the shades Tapestry, Damask, Ikat, and Brocade, which, appropriately enough for a silk-road product, may be "layered" and "intertwined" however one wishes. And don't forget their "East Meets West Nail Lacquer Collection" ($95 at Neiman Marcus).

Perhaps most people today know the silk road not through fashion, food, music, or politics, but through the massively multiplayer role-playing game "Silk Road Online": an abode of monsters and warriors where one undertakes quests and "arena battles" across a digital landscape stretching from China to Constantinople. But there are other Internet silk roads. More transgressive, but somehow appropriate, is the online marketplace where one can buy, for example, "Avatar acid"; "a gram of Afghani hash; 1/8th ounce of 'sour 13' weed; 14 grams of ecstasy; .1 grams tar heroin." There's no plutonium for sale, since the website prohibits sale of "anything whose purpose is to harm or defraud, such as stolen credit cards, assassinations, and weapons of mass destruction." One must access the site through the TOR network, which conceals participants' identity, and all purchases are made in the digital currency "bitcoin." But one can order with confidence from sellers rated by a system like that on Amazon and eBay and receive professionally packed deliveries in a few days. This underground online marketplace, too, is called "Silk Road."

While Central Eurasia has changed greatly, the commercial, biological, technological, and cultural communication that defined the silk road has only intensified in recent centuries—if anything, our modern era of globalization is itself defined by that intensification of exchange. We are living the logical conclusion of silk-road processes begun millennia ago. But the evocations of the silk road in music, travel, games, food, fashion, pharmaceuticals, and even politics speak to something else: nostalgia for a world connected but discrete, a world still capable of surprising us, where the bazaars at the next oasis sell something different from our own, where a strenuous journey yields a comparable measure of spiritual insight. That silk road may be a fantasy, but we still hope to travel it.

References

Chapter 1: Environment and empires

Ferdinand von Richthofen and first uses of "silk road": Ferdinand von Richthofen, "Über die zentralasiatischen Seidenstrassen bis zum 2. Jh. n. Chr." *Verhandlungen der Gesellschaft für Erdkunde zu Berlin* (1877), 96–122; Daniel C. Waugh, "From the Editor's Desktop: Richthofen's 'Silk Roads': Toward the Archaeology of a Concept," *The Silk Road* (online publication of the Silk Road Foundation) vol. 5, no. 1 (Summer 2007), 1–10. http://silkroadfoundation.org/newsletter/vol5num1/

"The places in between": Rory Stewart, *The Places in Between* (Orlando, FL: Harcourt, Inc., 2006).

Ecological zones of Central Eurasia: Denis Sinor, ed., "The Geographic Setting," in *The Cambridge History of Early Inner Asia* (Cambridge: Cambridge University Press, 1990), 19–38.

Ibn Khaldun's theory: Ibn Khaldun, *The Muqaddimah: An Introduction to History*, trans. and introduction by Franz Rosenthal; abridged and edited by N. J. Dawood (Princeton, NJ: Princeton University Press, 2005).

Gibbon's comments on character of Scythians and Tatars is in chap. 26 of his work: Edward Gibbon, *The History of the Decline and Fall of the Roman Empire*, ed. David Womersley (London: Penguin, 1995), vol. 2, 1025–26. Also available at http://www.gutenberg.org/files/732/732-h/732-h.htm.

On the socio-political organization of pastoral nomadic peoples: Joseph Fletcher, "The Mongols: Ecological and Social

Perspectives," *Harvard Journal of Asiatic Studies* 46:1 (June 1986): 11–50.

Sima Qian on the Xiongnu: Sima Qian, "The Account of the Xiongnu," *Records of the Grand Historian* (Shiji ch. 110), Han dynasty, vol. 2, trans. Burton Watson (New York: Columbia University Press, 1993), 129.

Ammianus Marcellinus on the Huns: Ammianus Marcellinus, *The Later Roman Empire (354–378)*, 31.2, ed. and trans. Walter Hamilton (Harmondsworth, UK: Penguin, 1986), 411–12.

Nicola Di Cosmo's argument regarding the Great Wall and nomad-type states: Nicola Di Cosmo, *Ancient China and Its Enemies: The Rise of Nomadic Power in East Asian History* (Cambridge: Cambridge University Press, 2002); Nicola Di Cosmo, "State Formation and Periodization in Inner Asian History," *Journal of World History* 10, no. 1 (1999): 1–40; "the first cry" quoted from 23.

Chapter 2: Eras of silk road fluorescence

"In our country there are no towns and no cultivated land . . .": Herodotus, Book 4, from *The Histories*, trans. Aubrey de Sélincourt (Harmondsworth, UK: Penguin Books, 1972), 312.

Nomad migrations and correlations between eastern and western history: Frederick John Teggart, *Rome and China: A Study of Correlations in History* (Berkeley: University of California Press, 1939).

Genghis Khan launching the Renaissance and comparison to Jesus: Jack Weatherford, *Genghis Khan and the Making of the Modern World* (New York: Three Rivers Press, 2004). The *Harper's* review of that book states "it's hard to think of anyone else who rose from such inauspicious beginnings to something so awesome, except maybe Jesus."

Qing and Russian Empires as Mongol successor states: Charles J. Halperin, *Russia and the Golden Horde: The Mongol Impact on Medieval Russian History* (Bloomington: Indiana University Press, 1985); Okada Hidehiro, "China as a Successor State to the Mongol Empire," in *The Mongol Empire and Its Legacy*, ed. Reuven Amitai-Preiss and David O. Morgan (Leiden: Brill, 1999), 260–72; Peter C. Perdue, *China Marches West: The Qing Conquest of Central Eurasia* (Cambridge, MA: Belknap Press of Harvard University Press, 2005).

Chapter 3: The biological silk road

Long-term trans-Eurasian exchange: Andrew Sherratt, "The Trans-Eurasian Exchange: The Pre-history of Chinese Relations with the West," in *Contact and Exchange in the Ancient World*, ed. Victor H. Mair (Honolulu: University of Hawai'i Press, 2006), 30–61.

William of Rubruck on "cosmos" (kumis): *The Journey of William of Rubruck to the Eastern Parts of the World, 1253–55, as narrated by himself, with two accounts of the earlier journey of John of Pian de Carpine*, trans. and ed. with an introductory notice by William Woodville Rockhill (London: Hakluyt Society, 1900); introduction and further annotation by Daniel Waugh, Silk Road Seattle, http://depts.washington.edu/silkroad/texts/rubruck.html. Quoted passage is from section V, "Kumiss," in Waugh's online version of the text.

Lactose intolerance/lactase persistence and Central Eurasians: "Got Lactase?" (2007), *Understanding Evolution* website, http://evolution.berkeley.edu/evolibrary/news/070401_lactose; Catherine J. E. Ingram, Charlotte A. Mulcare, Yuval Itan, Mark G. Thomas, and Dallas M. Swallow, "Lactose digestion and the Evolutionary Genetics of Lactase Persistence," *Human Genetics* 124, no. 6 (Jan. 2009): 579–91; Wang YG, Yan YS, Xu JJ, Du RF, S. D. Flatz, W. Kühnau, and G. Flatz, "Prevalence of Primary Adult Lactose Malabsorption in Three Populations of Northern China," *Human Genetics* 67, no. 1 (1984): 103–6.

Interbreeding of *Homo sapiens* and Neanderthals: Ker Than, "Neanderthals, Humans Interbred—First Solid DNA Evidence," published by the National Geographic Society, http://news.nationalgeographic.com/news/2010/05/100506-science-neanderthals-humans-mated-interbred-dna-gene/;
R. E. Green, J. Krause, A. W. Briggs, et al., "A Draft Sequence of the Neandertal Genome," *Science* 328, no. 5979 (May 2010): 710–22, http://www.eva.mpg.de/neandertal/press/presskit-neandertal/pdf/Science_Green.pdf.

DNA studies of silk road migrations: C. Lalueza-Fox, M. L. Sampietro, M. T. P. Gilbert, L. Castri, F. Facchini, D. Pettener, J. Bertranpetit, "Unravelling Migrations in the Steppe: Mitochondrial DNA Sequences from Ancient Central Asians," in *Proceedings: Biological Sciences*, vol. 271, no. 1542 (May 7, 2004): 941–47, published by The Royal Society, http://www.jstor.org/stable/4142653; Peter Forster, "Ice Ages and the Mitochondrial DNA Chronology of Human Dispersals: A Review," in "The Evolutionary Legacy of

the Ice Ages (Feb. 29, 2004): 255–64, special issue, http://www.
jstor.org/stable/4142177, *Philosophical Transactions: Biological
Sciences*, 359, no. 1442.

Mongol genetic marker on the Y chromosome: Tatiana Zerjal, Xue Yali;
Giorgio Bertorelle, R. Spencer Wells; Bao Weidong; Zhu Suling,
Raheel Qamar, Qasim Ayub, Aisha Mohyuddin, Fu Songbin, Li Pu,
Nadira Yuldasheva, Ruslan Ruzibakiev, Xu Jiujin, Shu Quangfang,
Du Ruofu, Yang Huangming, Matthew E. Hurles, and Elizabeth
Robinson, "The Genetic Legacy of the Mongols," *American Journal
of Human Genetics* 72, no. 3 (Mar. 2003): 717–22.

Mongols and plague: William H. McNeill, "The Impact of the Mongol
Empire on Shifting Disease Balances, 1200–1500," in *Plagues and
Peoples* (New York: Anchor Books, 1976, 1998), 132–75; George
D. Sussman, "Was the Black Death in India and China?" *Bulletin
of the History of Medicine* 85, no. 3 (Fall 2011): 319–55; Nicholas
Wade, "Europe's Plagues Came from China, Study Finds," *New York
Times*, Nov. 1, 2010, A10, http://www.nytimes.com/2010/11/01/
health/01plague.html; Giovanna Morelli et al., "*Yersina Pestis*
Genome Sequencing Identifies Patterns of Global Phylogenetic
Diversity," *Nature Genetics* 42 (2010): 1140–43, http://www.
nature.com/ng/journal/v42/n12/full/ng.705.html.

Horse domestication: David W. Anthony, *The Horse, The Wheel, and
Language: How Bronze-Age Riders from the Eurasian Steppes
Shaped the Modern World* (Princeton, NJ: Princeton University
Press, 2007).

Zhang Qian on blood-sweating horses: Sima Qian, *Shiji* (Records of
the Historian), ch. 123, "Dayuan liezhuan"; translation in Sima
Qian, "The Account of Dayuan," *Records of the Grand Historian*
(ch. 123), Han dynasty, vol. 2, trans. Burton Watson (New York:
Columbia University Press, 1993), 231–53.

Polo match in the *Shahnamah*: Ferdawsi, *The Epic of the Kings:
Shah-Nama, the National Epic of Persia*, trans. Reuben Levy
(London: Routledge and Kegan Paul, 1967), 97–98.

Schumpeter's theory of imperialism: Joseph A. Schumpeter, "The
Sociology of Imperialisms," in *Imperialism and Social Classes: Two
Essays* (New York: World Publishing, 1972), especially 141–42.

Alcoholic beverages in ancient Egypt and Mesopotamia: "Beer"
(vol. 1), "Wine" and "Intoxication" (vol. 2), in *The Oxford
Encyclopedia of Ancient Egypt*, ed. Donald B. Redforth (New York:
Oxford University Press, 2001); Alexander H. Joffe, "Alcohol and
Social Complexity in Ancient Western Asia," *Current*

Anthropology 39, no. 3 (June 1998): 297–322; Patrick E. McGovern, *Ancient Wine: The Search for the Origins of Viniculture* (Princeton, NJ: Princeton University Press, 2003); John Varriano, *Wine: A Cultural History* (London: Reaktion, 2010).

Herodotus on wine among Persians and Scythians: Herodotus, *The Histories*, trans. Aubrey de Sélincourt (Harmondsworth, UK: Penguin, 1972), 1:133 on Persian deliberations and 4:70 on Scythians drinking wine with blood.

Strabo on wine in Central Eurasia: Strabo, *The Geography of Strabo*, ed. and trans. H. L. Jones (Cambridge, MA: Harvard University Press, 1924), 11:10.

Grapes and wine in China: Li Zhengping, *Chinese Wine* (Cambridge: Cambridge University Press, 2010); E. H. Schafer, *The Golden Peaches of Samarkand: A Study of T'ang Exotics* (Berkeley: University of California Press, 1963), 141–45; Lü Guang in Kucha: Valerie Hansen, *The Silk Road: A New History* (Oxford: Oxford University Press, 2012), 68; Li Fang, *Taiping yulan*, 125:604 as cited in *Shiliuguo chunqiu* and in Éric Trombert, *On Ikeda*, and Guangda Zhang, *Les manuscrits chinois de Koutcha: Fonds Pelliot de la Bibliothèque Nationale de France* (Paris: Institut des hautes études chinoises du Collège de France, 2000), 11.

Xuanzang . . . at the Western Turk Yabghu's camp: Huili, *Datang daciensi Sanzang fashi chuan*, j. 2. *Taisho Tripitaka* vol. 50, no. 2053 (CBETA Chinese Electronic Tripitaka V1.29, Normalized Version, T50n2053_p0227b14-T50n2053_p0227b15).

"Fine grape wine, a jade cup gleaming in the moonlight": My translation of Wang Han's *Liangzhou ci*, cf. Stephen Owen, *The Poetry of the Early T'ang* (New Haven: Yale University Press, 1977).

Wine consumption in China today: "China becomes biggest export market for Bordeaux wine outside EU," *Telegraph* Mar. 11, 2010, http://www.telegraph.co.uk/foodanddrink/wine/7423067/China-becomes-biggest-export-market-for-bordeaux-wine-outside-EU.html#.' Lucy Evans, "China and the World Wine Market," Food Editorials.com (2010), http://www.streetdirectory.com/food_editorials/beverages/wine/china_and_the_world_wine_market.html; Syrah Suen, "China's Wine Consumption Expected to Boom in 2010" *China wine online*, http://www.winechina.com/en/read.asp?id=2010011414.

"Wine-ode" of Ibn al-Fārid: Ibn al-Farid, trans. and intro. by Th. Emil Homerin, Michael A. Sells, preface, *'Umar Ibn al-Farid: Sufi Verse, Saintly Life* (New York: Paulist Press, 2001), 47–51.

Hafiz, "Hair disheveled": I have used the translation of *ghazal* 26
(Qazvini-Ghani enumeration) by Reza Saberi, in *Poems of Hafez*
(Lanham, MD: University Press of America, 1995), 20–21; for
clarity, I made one slight change in the translation with reference to
the nineteenth-century translation by H. Wilberforce Clarke (who
numbers this *ghazal* 44), replacing Saberi's "narcissus" with "eye" as
used by Clarke and other translators.

Silver drinks fountain in the Mongol court: *The Journey of William
of Rubruck to the Eastern parts of the World, 1253–55, as narrated
by himself, with two accounts of the earlier journey of John of Pian
de Carpine*, trans. from the Latin and ed., with an introductory
note by William Woodville Rockhill (London: Hakluyt Society,
1900); introduction and further annotation by Daniel Waugh, Silk
Road Seattle, sec. 15, http://depts.washington.edu/silkroad/texts/
rubruck.html.

Trans-Eurasian crop exchanges: Thomas T. Allsen, *Culture
and Conquest in Mongol Eurasia* (Cambridge: Cambridge
University Press, 2001); Berthold Laufer, *Sino-Iranica: Chinese
Contributions to the History of Civilization in Ancient Iran, with
Special Reference to the History of Cultivated Plants and Products*
(New York: Klaus Reprint Corp., 1967; Taipei: Cheng-wen, 1967);
Joseph Needham and Francesca Bray, *Science and Civilization
in China*, vol. 6, pt. 2 (Cambridge: Cambridge University Press,
1984); J. Smartt and N. W. Simmonds, *Evolution of Crop Plants*.
2nd ed. (Essex, UK: Longman Scientific and Technical, 1995); J. G.
Vaughan and C. A. Geissler, *The New Oxford Book of Food Plants*
(Oxford: Oxford University Press, 1997).

Dumplings: Holly Chase, "The Meyhane or McDonalds? Changes in
Eating Habits and the Evolution of Fast Food in Istanbul," in *A
Taste of Thyme: Culinary Cultures of the Middle East*, 2nd ed., ed.
Sami Zubaida and Richard Tapper (London: Tauris Parke, 2000),
81; Josh Wilson with Andrei Nesterov, "Pelmeni: A Tasty History,"
Newsletter of SRAS (School of Russian and Asian Studies) Jan. 10,
2010, http://www.sras.org/news2.php?m=287.

Chapter 4: The technological silk road

The chair and cane sugar: John Kieschnick, *The Impact of Buddhism
on Chinese Material Culture* (Princeton, NJ: Princeton University
Press, 2003), chap. 4.

"Trans-ecological" and "trans-civilizational" trade: David Christian,

"Silk Roads of Steppe Roads? The Silk Roads in World History," in *Realms of the Silk Roads: Ancient and Modern*, Silk Road Studies 4, ed. David Christian and Craig Benjamin (Turnhout, Belgium: Brepols, 2000), 67–94.

Classical references to silk: Virgil, *Georgics* 2:120–120; Strabo, *Geography* 15.1.21; Pliny the Elder, *Natural History* 6.20, trans. from Pliny the Elder; *The Natural History of Pliny*, trans. John Bostock and H. T. Riley (London: H. G. Bohn, 1855–57); Lucan, *Pharsalia*, 10.141, *The Periplus of the Erythraean Sea: Travel and Trade in the Indian Ocean by a Merchant of the First Century*, trans. William H. Schoff (New York: Longmans, Green, 1912), 265; Seneca, *De Beneficiis* 7.9, trans. from *Southern Literary Messenger* 2, no. 1 (Dec. 1835): 355. All classical texts and some translations available online at http://www.perseus.tufts.edu.

"Sons of poor families": Sima Qian, *Shiji*, bk. 123, "Dayuan liezhuan," trans. Burton Watson, *Records of the Grand Historian*, rev. ed., Han dynasty. vol. 2 (New York: Columbia University Press, 1993), 242.

Mughal trade of textiles for horses: Scott Levi, "India, Russia and the Eighteenth-Century Transformation of the Central Asian Caravan Trade," *Journal of the Economic and Social History of the Orient* 42 no. 4 (1999): 519–48.

Paper and printing in China and Islamic world: Jonathan M. Bloom, *Paper before Print: The History and Impact of Paper in the Islamic World* (New Haven, CT: Yale University Press, 2001); Jonathan M. Bloom, "Silk Road or Paper Road?" *The Silkroad Foundation Newsletter* 3, no. 2 (Dec. 2005), http://www.silk-road.com/ newsletter/vol3num2/5_bloom.php.

Chinese background for the European invention of typography: Tsien Tsuen-Hsuin in *Science and Civilisation in China*, ed. Joseph Needham and Tsien Tsuen-Hsuin, vol. 5, pt. 1, *Paper and Printing* (Cambridge: Cambridge University Press, 1985).

Eurasian medical tradition and humoral theory: Thomas Allsen, *Culture and Conquest in Mongol Eurasia*, chap. 16, "Medicine" (Cambridge: Cambridge University Press, 2001), 141–61; E. N. Anderson, *The Food of China* (New Haven, CT: Yale University Press, 1990); Mary Hardy, Ian Coulter, Swamy Venuturupalli, Elizabeth A. Roth, Joya Favreau, Sally C. Morton, and Paul Shekelle, "Appendix A. Ayurveda's History, Beliefs and Practices," in "Ayurvedic Interventions for Diabetes Mellitus: A Systematic Review," Report No. 01-E040, *Evidence Reports/Technology*

Assessments, no. 41 (Rockville, MD: Agency for Healthcare Research and Quality, Sept. 2001), http://www.ncbi.nlm.nih.gov/books/NBK33781; Paul U. Unschuld, *Medicine in China: A History of Ideas* (Berkeley: University of California Press, 1985).

Donkey meat: "Donkey meat: the most traditional way to get a piece of ass," *People's Daily Online*, Mar. 30, 2010, http://english.peopledaily.com.cn/90001/90782/6935139.html.

Smallpox: Joseph Needham, *Science and Civilisation in China*, vol. 6, pt. 6, sec. 44, "Medicine" (Cambridge: Cambridge University Press, 1984), 127–53; William J. Broad and Judith Miller, "Report Provides New Details of Soviet Smallpox Accident," *New York Times*, June 15, 2002.

Nuclear weapons: Sergei Goncharenko, "Sino-Soviet Military Cooperation," in *Brothers in Arms: The Rise and Fall of the Sino-Soviet Alliance, 1945–1963*, ed. Odd Arne Westad (Washington, DC: Woodrow Wilson Center Press; Stanford, CA: Stanford University Press, 1998).

Gunpowder: Robert K. G. Temple, *The Genius of China: 3,000 Years of Science, Discovery and Invention* (New York: Simon & Schuster, 1986), 224–48.

The chariot: David W. Anthony, *The Horse, The Wheel, and Language: How Bronze-Age Riders from the Eurasian Steppes Shaped the Modern World* (Princeton, NJ: Princeton University Press, 2007), 397–411 and 460–63; Edward L. Shaughnessy, "Historical Perspectives on the Introduction of the Chariot into China" *Harvard Journal of Asiatic Studies* 48, no. 1 (Jun. 1988): 189–237.

Chapter 5: The arts on the silk road

Eurasian story exchanges: Richard Francis Burton, trans., "The Tale of the Husband and the Parrot," in *The Book of The Thousand Nights and a Night*, 6 vols. (New York: Heritage Press, 1934), vol. 1; Walter Cohen, "Eurasian Fiction," *Global South* 1, nos. 1 and 2 (2007): 100–119; E. B. Cowell, ed., *The Jātaka: Or Stories of the Buddha's Former Births*, trans. from the Pāli by various hands, 6 vols. (Cambridge: Cambridge University Press, 1895–1907; repr., London: Routledge and Kegan Paul, 1973). I refer to the following stories from the *Jātaka*: vol. 1 #189, #294, #145; vol. 2 #198, #208, #294. James Huntley Grayson, "Rabbit Visits the Dragon Palace: A Korea-Adapted, Buddhist Tale from India," *Fabula* 45, no. 1/2 (Berlin: 2004); 69–93; Heading essay on *Jakata* tales in Sarah

Lawall, ed., *The Norton Anthology of World Literature* (New York: W. W. Norton, 2002), vol. A.; Victor H. Mair, *Tun-huang Popular Narratives* (Cambridge: Cambridge University Press, 1983); *The Norton Anthology of Literature* (online), Discovery Module 14, "The sharing of narrative materials in the Middle Ages," http://www.wwnorton.com/college/english/worldlit2e/full/discovery_modules/dm14_1.htm; Visnu Sarma, *The Pancatantra*, trans. with an intro. by Chandra Rajan (London: Penguin, 1993).

Lutes: Stephen Blum, "Central Asia," in *Grove Music Online. Oxford Music Online*, http://0-www.oxfordmusiconline.com.library.lausys.georgetown.edu/subscriber/article/grove/music/05284; Jean During, "Barbat" in *Encyclopaedia Iranica* (1988), http://www.iranica.com/articles/barbat. J.-Cl. Chabrier, A. Dietrich, C. E. Bosworth, H. G. Farmer, "ʿŪd," *Encyclopaedia of Islam*, 2nd ed. (Brill, 2011), http://www.brillonline.nl/subscriber/entry?entry=islam_COM-1270; print version: vol. 10, 767, col. 2; H. G. Farmer, "Ud," in *New Grove Dictionary of Music and Musicians*, Oxford: Oxford University Press, 1980; C. Marcel-Dubois, *Les instruments de musique de l'Inde ancienne* (Presses universitaires de France, 1941), 89, 205; T. S. Vyzgo, *Muzykal'nye instrumenty Sredneĭ Azii* (Musical Instruments of Central Asia) (Moscow, 1980); O. Wright, "Mūsīkī, later Mūsīḳā," *Encyclopaedia of Islam*, 2nd ed. (Leiden: Brill, 2011), http://www.brillonline.nl/subscriber/entry?entry=islam_COM-0812; print version: vol. 7, 681, col. 1.

Muqam: "China IV: Living Traditions: Northwest China" in *Grove Music Online. Oxford Music Online*, s.v. "China," ed. Alan R. Thrasher et al., http://0-www.oxfordmusiconline.com.library.lausys.georgetown.edu/subscriber/article/grove/music/43141pg4; Rachel Harris, *The Making of a Musical Canon in Chinese Central Asia: The Uyghur Twelve Muqam* (Farnham, Surrey: Ashgate, 2008); Nathan Light, *Intimate Heritage: Creating Uyghur Muqam Song in Xinjiang* (Berlin: LIT Verlag, 2008).

Halos: E. H. Ramsden, "The Halo: A Further Enquiry into Its Origin," *Burlington Magazine for Connoisseurs* 78, no. 457 (Apr. 1941): 123–27, 131.

The three hares: "The Three Hares Project," http://www.chrischapmanphotography.co.uk/hares/index.html; "The Travels of the Three Rabbits: Shared Iconography Across the Silk Road," *IDP News*, no. 18 (International Dunhuang Project, Summer 2001), http://idp.bl.uk/archives/news18/idpnews_18.a4d.

Persian miniatures: Sheila Blair, "East Meets West Under the Mongols," http://www.silk-road.com/newsletter/vol3num2/6_blair.php; Sheila S. Blair and Jonathan M. Bloom, *The Art and Architecture of Islam 1250–1800* (New Haven, CT: Yale University Press, 1994); J. P. Losty et al., "Indian subcontinent," in *Grove Art Online. Oxford Art Online*, http://www.oxfordartonline.com/subscriber/article/grove/art/T040113pg20.

Blue-and-white ware: John Carswell, *Blue and White: Chinese Porcelain and Its Impact on the Western World* (Chicago: David and Alfred Smart Gallery, University of Chicago, 1985); John Carswell, *Blue and White: Chinese Porcelain around the World* (Chicago: Art Media Resources, 2000); William R. Sargent, "Blue-and-white ceramic," in *Grove Art Online, Oxford Art Online*, http://0-www.oxfordartonline.com.library.lausys.georgetown.edu/subscriber/article/grove/art/T009347.

Chapter 6: Whither the silk road?

Early modern continuation of the silk road: James A. Millward, *Eurasian Crossroads: A History of Xinjiang* (New York: Columbia University Press, 2008), 72–76; Scott Levi, "India, Russia and the Eighteenth-Century Transformation of the Central Asian Caravan Trade," *Journal of the Economic and Social History of the Orient* 42, no. 4 (1999): 519–48.

Kazakh-Qing silk trade in eighteenth and nineteenth centuries: The documents referenced are in the No. One Historical Archive in Beijing; discussion in James Millward, *Beyond the Pass: Economy, Ethnicity and Empire in Qing Central Asia, 1759–1864* (Stanford, CA: Stanford University Press, 1998), 45–48.

Zhang Yin's Jiulong company: "China's richest woman: from waste to wealth," *Xinhua* via *China Daily*, Oct. 20, 2006, http://www.chinadaily.com.cn/china/2006-10/20/content_713250.htm.

Hillary Clinton's silk road initiative: "Secretary of State Hillary Rodham Clinton on India and the United States: A Vision for the 21st Century," July 20, 2011, Anna Centenary Library, Chennai, India, http://iipdigital.usembassy.gov/st/english/texttrans/2011/07/2011 0720165044su0.7134014.html#axzz1SiHYG012.

Iranian, Pakistani, and Chinese political use of the "silk road" idea: "Iran, China Urge Stronger Ties." PressTV, Aug. 20, 2011, http://www.presstv.ir/detail/194884.html; "Sino-pak Ties: 'Silk Road Will Be Fully Revived," *Express Tribune*, Sept. 3, 2011, http://tribune.

com.pk/story/243971/sino-pak-ties-silk-road-will-be-fully-revived/;
Li Xiguang, "Fuxing sichou zhi lu, dapo meiguo weidu" (Revive the
silk road, smash American containment), *Huanqiu shibao*, Nov. 28,
2011, http://opinion.huanqiu.com/roll/2011-11/2214092.html.

"Silk-road inspired regional American cuisine": from the website of
the restaurant Mie N Yu, http://www.mienyu.com/information.
cfm.

Silk road in fashion: Hilary Alexander, "Oscar de la Renta autumn/
winter 2011 at New York Fashion Week." *Telegraph*, Feb. 16,
2011, http://fashion.telegraph.co.uk/columns/hilary-alexander/
TMG8329386/Oscar-de-la-Renta-autumnwinter-2011-at-New-
York-Fashion-Week.html; "Le Metier de Beauté Fall/Winter
2011 Collection: Silk Road," *Temptalia Beauty Blog*, http://www.
temptalia.com/le-metier-de-beaute-fallwinter-2011-collection-
silk-road.

Online silk road marketplace: Adrian Chen, "The Underground
Website Where You Can Buy Any Drug Imaginable," *Gawker*, June
6, 2011, http://gawker.com/5805928/the-underground-website-
where-you-can-buy-any-drug-imaginable.

Further reading

Adshead, S. A. M. *Central Asia in World History*. New York:
St. Martin's, 1993.

Allsen, Thomas T. *Culture and Conquest in Mongol Eurasia*.
Cambridge: Cambridge University Press, 2001.

Anthony, David W. *The Horse, The Wheel, and Language: How
Bronze-Age Riders from the Eurasian Steppes Shaped the Modern
World*. Princeton, NJ: Princeton University Press, 2007.

Barfield, Thomas. *The Perilous Frontier: Nomadic Empires and China*.
Cambridge, MA: Basil Blackwell, 1989.

Beckwith, Christopher I. *Empires of the Silk Road*. Princeton,
NJ: Princeton University Press, 2009.

Beckwith, Christopher I. *The Tibetan Empire in Central Asia*.
Princeton, NJ: Princeton University Press, 1987.

Bonavia, Judy. *The Silk Road: Retracing the Ancient Trade Route*.
Lincolnwood, IL: Passport Books, 1988.

Boulnois, Luce et al. *The Silk Road: Monks, Warriors and Merchants*.
New York: W. W. Norton, 2004; Hong Kong: Odyssey, 2005.

Carrère d'Encausse, Hélène. *L'empire d'Eurasie: Une histoire de
l'empire russe de 1552 à nos jours*. Paris: Fayard, 2005.

Christian, David. *A History of Russia, Central Asia and Mongolia*.
Vol. 1, *Inner Eurasia from Prehistory to the Mongol Empire*.
Oxford: Blackwell, 1998.

Christian, David. "Inner Eurasia as a Unit of World History." *Journal of
World History* 5.2 (1994): 73–211.

Christian, David. "Silk Roads of Steppe Roads? The Silk Roads in
World History." In *Realms of the Silk Roads: Ancient and Modern*,

Silk Road Studies 4, edited by David Christian and Craig Benjamin. Turnhout, Belgium: Brepols, 2000, 67–94.

Dawson, Christopher, ed. *Mission to Asia: Narratives and Letters of the Franciscan Missionaries in Mongolia and China in the Thirteenth and Fourteenth Centuries*. Translated by a nun of Stanbrook Abbey. New York: Harper & Row, 1966.

Di Cosmo, Nicola, ed. *The Cambridge History of Inner Asia—The Chinggisid Age*. New York: Cambridge University Press, 2009.

Edwardes, M. *East-West Passage: The Travel of Ideas, Arts and Inventions between Asia and the Western World*. New York: Taplinger, 1971.

Evtuhov, Catherine, David Goldfrank, Lindsey Hughes, and Richard Stites. *A History of Russia: Peoples, Legends, Events, Forces*. Boston: Houghton Mifflin, 2004.

Forbes, Richard. *Religions of the Silk Road: Overland Trade and Cultural Exchange from Antiquity to the Fifteenth Century*. New York: St. Martin's Griffin, 1999.

Franck, Irene, and David Brownstone. *The Silk Road: A History*. New York: Facts on File, 1986.

Frank, André Gunder. *The Centrality of Central Asia*. Comparative Asian Studies 8. Amsterdam: V.U. University Press, 1992.

Golden, Peter B. *Central Asia in World History*. New York: Oxford University Press, 2011.

Golden, Peter B. "Nomads and Sedentary Societies in Medieval Eurasia." Edited by Michael Adas. Washington, DC: American Historical Association, 1998.

Halperin, Charles J. *Russia and the Golden Horde: The Mongol Impact on Medieval Russian History*. Bloomington: Indiana University Press, 1985.

Hansen, Valerie. *The Silk Road: A New History*. New York: Oxford University Press, 2012.

History of Civilizations of Central Asia. 6 vols. Paris: UNESCO, 1992–2005.

Hobson, John M. *The Eastern Origins of Western Civilization*. Cambridge: Cambridge University Press, 2004.

Holt, Frank Lee. *Alexander the Great and Bactria: The Formation of a Greek Frontier in Central Asia*. Leiden: Brill, 1988.

Hopkirk, Peter. *Foreign Devils on the Silk Road: The Search for the Lost Cities and Treasures of Chinese Central Asia*. London: John Murray, 1980.

Khazanov, A. M. *Nomads and the Outside World.* Translated by Julia Crookenden. 2nd ed. Madison: University of Wisconsin Press, 1983.

Knobloch, Edgar. *Beyond the Oxus: Archaeology, Art, and Architecture of Central Asia.* London: Ernest Benn, 1972.

Komaroff, Linda, and Stefano Carboni. *The Legacy of Genghis Khan: Courtly Art and Culture in Western Asia, 1256–1353.* New York: Metropolitan Museum of Art; New Haven, CT: Yale University Press, 2002.

La Vaissière, Étienne de. *Sogdian Traders: A History.* Translated by James Ward. Leiden, Boston: Brill, 2005.

Larner, John. *Marco Polo and the Discovery of the World.* New Haven, CT: Yale University Press, 1999.

Laufer, Berthold. *Sino-Iranica: Chinese Contributions to the History of Civilization in Ancient Iran, with Special Reference to the History of Cultivated Plants and Products.* Chicago: Field Museum of Natural History, 1919. Repr. New York: Kraus, 1967. Repr. Taipei: Cheng-wen, 1967.

Levi, Scott, and Ron Sela, eds. *Islamic Central Asia: An Anthology of Historical Sources.* Bloomington: Indiana University Press, 2010.

Liu, Xinru. *Ancient India and Ancient China: Trade and Religious Exchanges, AD 1–600.* New Delhi: Oxford University Press, 1988.

Liu, Xinru. *Silk and Religion: An Exploration of Material Life and the Thought of People, AD 600–1200.* New Delhi: Oxford University Press, 1996.

Liu, Xinru. *The Silk Road in World History.* New York: Oxford University Press, 2010.

Mallory, J. P. *In Search of the Indo-Europeans: Language, Archaeology, and Myth.* London: Thames & Hudson, 1989.

Mallory, J. P., and Victor Mair. *The Tarim Mummies: Ancient China and the Mystery of the Earliest Peoples from the West.* New York: Thames & Hudson, 2000.

Millward, James A. *Eurasian Crossroads: A History of Xinjiang.* New York: Columbia University Press, 2008.

Morgan, David. *The Mongols.* Cambridge, MA: Blackwell, 1990.

Sariandi, Victor. *The Golden Horde of Bactria.* New York: Abrams, 1985.

Schafer, E. H. *The Golden Peaches of Samarkand: A Study of T'ang Exotics.* Berkeley: University of California Press, 1963.

Sinor, Dennis, ed. *The Cambridge History of Early Inner Asia.* Cambridge: Cambridge University Press, 1990.

Soucek, Svat. *A History of Inner Asia*. Cambridge: Cambridge University Press, 2000.

Temple, Robert K. G. *The Genius of China: 3,000 Years of Science, Discovery, and Invention*. New York: Simon & Schuster, 1986.

Thorday, Lazlo. *Mounted Archers: The Beginnings of Central Asian History*. Seattle: University of Washington Press, 1998.

Weatherford, Jack. *Genghis Khan and the Making of the Modern World*. New York: Crown, 2004.

Whitfield, Roderick, Susan Whitfield, and Neville Agnew. *Cave Temples of Mogao: Art and History on the Silk Road*. Los Angeles: Getty Conservation Institute and the J. Paul Getty Museum, 2000.

Whitfield, Susan. *Life Along the Silk Road*. London: John Murray, 1999.

Whitfield, Susan, and Ursula Sims-Williams. *The Silk Road: Trade, Travel, War, and Faith*. London: British Library, 2004.

Wood, Frances. *Did Marco Polo Go to China?* Boulder, CO: Westview, 1996.

Wood, Frances. *The Silk Road: 2000 Years in the Heart of Asia*. Berkeley: University of California Press, 2002.

Wriggins, Sally Hovey. *Xuanzang: Buddhist Pilgrim on the Silk Road*. Boulder, CO: Westview, 2004.

Websites

The Silk Road Project
http://www.silkroadproject.org/
Founded by Yo-Yo Ma in 1998, the Silk Road Project promotes
    contemporary arts and educational activities inspired by the
    silk road. The website includes many educational materials,
    particularly regarding instruments and music.

The Silk Road—The Virtual Labs Project at Stanford
http://virtuallabs.stanford.edu/silkroad/SilkRoad.html
Interactive maps, images and music clips.

Silk Road Seattle
http://depts.washington.edu/silkroad/
A trove of geographic, artistic, architectural images, and other
    resources. Particularly helpful is the collection of silk-road-related
    public domain primary texts in translation.

The Silk Road Foundation Newsletter / Silk Road Journal
http://www.silkroadfoundation.org/toc/newsletter.html
Illustrated online and downloadable journal with accessible articles by
    experts on all aspects of silk road history and culture, expansively
    defined.

Index

Note: Page numbers in *italics* indicate images.

Index